General Knowledge
and Arts Education

General Knowledge and Arts Education

An Interpretation of
E. D. Hirsch's *Cultural Literacy*

RALPH A. SMITH

University of Illinois Press   Urbana and Chicago

Chapter 5 of this book first appeared in *Arts Education Policy Review* 94 (March–
April 1993), 2–18, and is reprinted with the permission of the Helen Dwight
Reid Educational Foundation. Published by Heldref Publications, 1319 18th
Street, N.W., Washington, DC, 20036-1892. Copyright 1993.

Library of Congress Cataloging-in-Publication Data
Smith, Ralph Alexander.
    General knowledge and arts education : an interpretation of E.D.
Hirsch's Cultural literacy / Ralph A. Smith.
        p.   cm.
    Includes index.
    ISBN 0-252-02119-3. — ISBN 0-252-06406-2 (pbk.)
        1. Arts—Study and teaching—United States—History—20th century.
    2. Hirsch, E. D. (Eric Donald), 1928-   Cultural literacy.
    3. Educational anthropology—United States.   4. Multiculturalism—
    United States.   I. National Arts Education Research Center (U.S.)
    II. Title.
    NX304.A1S65   1994   93-50825
    700'.7'0973—dc20   CIP

To E. D. Hirsch, Jr., whose concern
for a higher level of national literacy
was the inspiration for this study.

Contents

Preface   ix

ONE   The Tradition of General Knowledge   1

TWO   Hirsch on Cultural Literacy   7

THREE   The Reception of *Cultural Literacy*   29

FOUR   The Arts and Contextual Knowledge   45

FIVE   The Question of Multiculturalism   79

SIX   The Arts, General Knowledge, and Curriculum   109

Notes   143

Index   153

Preface

General Knowledge and Arts Education is a product of a study on cultural literacy and arts education sponsored by the National Arts Education Research Center located at the University of Illinois at Urbana-Champaign. The first product was a special issue of the *Journal of Aesthetic Education* (Spring 1990), which was devoted to discussions of cultural literacy and arts education by E. D. Hirsch, Jr., and a number of specialists in educational theory, dance, music, theater, literature, the visual arts, art history, and the philosophy of art. The special issue was later published as a book, *Cultural Literacy and Arts Education*. The contents of the volume are discussed in chapter 4. The occasion for the study was the publication of Hirsch's *Cultural Literacy: What Every American Needs to Know* in 1987, which was updated and expanded in 1988.

The purpose of the special issue and the first book of the cultural literacy study was neither to feature a critique of Hirsch's ideas nor to suggest further additions to his word list. Rather, the aim was to draw attention to what seems unquestionable today—the serious shrinkage of background knowledge and information that people bring to their efforts to communicating with and understanding one another. On the assumption that such shrinkage has also occurred in basic knowledge about the arts, it seemed worthwhile to address the question of cultural literacy in arts education in regard to what teachers of art education and those who prepare them need to know and what learners in the schools need to be taught. Indeed, it may well be that the teaching of art provides an even more obvious instance of what Hirsch has criticized as a content-neutral method of teaching general skills. The contributors to

Cultural Literacy and Arts Education were therefore asked to identify the contextual information that is important for understanding and appreciating works of art. How, for example, does such knowledge help to reveal rather than obscure the character and substance of artworks?

The study at hand presents an interpretation of cultural literacy from the standpoint of one with interests in the problems of justifying the study of the arts in the schools and the definition of cultural and educational relations. I point out some antecedents of Hirsch's concerns and discuss his key ideas, their reception by various groups, and their significance for a curriculum of arts education. Given the attention that the topic of multiculturalism has received, the question of its relevance to cultural literacy will be singled out for extended commentary.

Acknowledgments

Particular thanks are due to Jack McKenzie, dean emeritus of the College of Fine and Applied Arts at the University of Illinois at Urbana-Champaign, who was the National Arts Education Research Center's managing director during the period of the study, and to Charles Leonhard, professor emeritus of music and the center's director of research, for their belief in the importance of a study of cultural literacy and arts education. Warren Neuman, the director of the arts education program of the National Endowment for the Arts during the period of the study, also provided encouragement. A large debt, of course, is owed to E. D. Hirsch, Jr., and I further wish to thank Penelope McKeon of the City Arts Institute of Sydney, Australia, for her helpful research assistance. Readers of an earlier draft of the study made a number of helpful suggestions that have improved the text, and I thank them as well.

CHAPTER ONE

The Tradition
of General Knowledge

FOR AN ORATION delivered at the London School of Economics and Political Science in December of 1961, E. H.
Gombrich, the distinguished art historian and psychologist, selected for
his topic "The Tradition of General Knowledge."[1] The purpose of the
oration was to explore the link between a society's shared knowledge
and shared values. It will become evident that Gombrich's speech has a
bearing on E. D. Hirsch's interpretation of cultural literacy and anticipates his thesis in some important respects.

Gombrich begins by recalling an Agatha Christie story in which at
a cocktail party at Claridge's, a character committed a gaffe that ultimately led to her being unmasked as a murderess. This character mis-
takenly thought that a reference made to the Judgment of Paris implied
a judgment about the relative merits of Paris, France. But Paris, she pro-
claimed to those assembled, does not cut any ice nowadays compared
to London and New York. Well, observes Gombrich, at Claridge's it
pays to know your classical mythology, or at least a smidgen of it; such
knowledge just might keep you beyond the reach of the law.

Gombrich uses this fictional episode to indicate how little bits of information enable one to participate effectively in society, or, in the case
of Christie's story, in a certain social class. To be sure, Gombrich has
no use for snobbishness, for the expression of disdain toward those who
don't share one's beliefs and values. But he does set store by the tradition of general knowledge which, he thinks, has diminished nearly to the
point of disappearance.

What does Gombrich mean by "general knowledge"? Consider, he asks, what would count as general knowledge about the meaning of the Judgment of Paris, an incident in classical mythology that ultimately brought on the Trojan War. It may be comforting to some readers to be told that Gombrich, one of the most distinguished scholars of our time, admits to having quite a limited understanding of the incident. He recalls that he was young when he came across mention of it in a potted version of Greek legends, but didn't learn anything more until after he noticed representations of it in the works of many painters, for example, in the painting by Rubens in the National Gallery (a case, one might say, of not having read the original story but having seen pictures of it). From this recollection Gombrich concludes that general information can be quite serviceable even when it is vague and incomplete, indeed when it is nothing more than rumor and hearsay and thus not really knowledge in the strict sense at all. "Nobody," he writes, "who calls an art quixotic or compares a scene with Dante's Inferno wants to imply that he has read Cervantes or studied the *Divine Comedy*. He simply uses a common coin which he knows to be current." [2] But effective social communication breaks down when the response to a reference to "sour grapes" is a discourse on the glucose content of fruit.

We all know what Gombrich means: All living languages presuppose some sharing of knowledge, and all cultures have a common stock of information on which their members rely for effective communication. The items making up such knowledge are not necessarily ones that society especially reveres or cherishes; they simply help us to communicate and understand one another. From Gombrich's own remembrance of how he came to know about the Judgment of Paris, it is apparent that the history of art is a valuable source of general knowledge. It is one of several fields of common knowledge that Gombrich calls "sources of metaphor." Try, he says, to understand Indian poetry and literature, Islamic culture, or a British parliamentary debate without any inkling of what a cow means to an Indian villager's life and worship, without some knowledge of the Koran, and a recollection of *Alice's Adventures in Wonderland*. Religion, of course, provides most cultures with a central domain of metaphor; religious metaphors, moreover, typically survive the decline of faith. Where, asks Gombrich, would European poetry be without Venus and Mars, Cupid's dart, and Jove's thunderbolt, not to mention biblical references? Many of these metaphors are learned in childhood and become assimilated into one's flesh and bones. The importance of this learning by assimilation was realized as early as classical antiquity, which emphasized rhetoric and oratory. Persons considered articulate had internalized sources of metaphor that enabled them to tap the core of shared images, feelings, and memories. But with the decline of the rhetorical tradition, the question of what general knowledge should consist of became more difficult to answer.

What should constitute general knowledge, or sources of metaphor, for people living today? Gombrich thinks that an answer to this question will not be found in arguments from relevance and usefulness in the sense that a telephone book is useful. To be in the swim of culture, he says, and not merely in the swim of society, there is nothing more valuable for Westerners than the study of the classics of Western civilization. It is not only that such study has a special capacity to discipline the mind—the study of the classics of other civilizations can also do that—but it also provides access to useful reservoirs, or pools of metaphor, into which one can dip when trying to understand or explain something. The symbols, ideas, and situations of classical mythology transcend the more commonplace sources of metaphor through their concern with perennial human problems. Most certainly they have helped to shape civilization itself for those who live in the West. The Athenian and Spartan images of life are enduring possibilities for interpreting our moral obligations, as are the Apollonian and Dionysian alternatives. And we still speak of draconian laws, stoic endurance, epicurean living, and cynical indifference. The influence of the language of Shakespeare, of course, is immeasurable.

Of moment here is Gombrich's discussion of areas of cultural metaphor. He says that artists are "lasting embodiments of human greatness, its triumphs and temptations. Michelangelo and Raphael, Rubens and Rembrandt, Van Gogh and Cézanne are not only objects of art-historical study or investments or status symbols for collectors. They are centers of attraction and repulsion to be loved, admired, criticized or rejected, living forces with which we get involved. They are culture heroes, Gods of our secular pantheon, beneficent or baleful, serene or capricious, but like Gods they must be approached with respect and humility for they can light up for us whole areas of the mind which would have been dark without them." To study Raphael today, for example, is not merely to see him as a historical figure or to estimate the capacity of his works to provide significant aesthetic experiences, "but to examine our own relation to ideal beauty" (15-16). Works of art enable us

to examine our relation to many other spheres of human experience—
love, courage, humility, death, victory, and defeat. This use of works of
art, in other words, is central to traditional justifications for education
in the humanities. Gombrich laments the fact that the symbols, images,
allusions, and associations we know as the Western cultural heritage are
"receding from our grasp as so many bridges to the past become im-
passable" (4). The problem is how to restore these bridges to use.

Gombrich realizes that any effort to convey general knowledge at
the college or university level will be resisted by the modern penchant
for specialized studies. Perhaps typical of the traditional scholar's attitude toward specialized as opposed to general knowledge is a remark by
another great art historian, Erwin Panofsky, who once said that at its
beginning the new discipline of art history had to disentangle itself not
only from practical art instruction and art appreciation, but also from
"that amorphous monster 'general education.'"[3] Gombrich nevertheless observes that those who dismiss general education as superficial are
often the same ones who express dismay at the astonishing thinness of
their undergraduates' general knowledge. The solution to this problem,
however, does not lie in remedial courses in general knowledge during the college years, but in a curriculum of general education in the
schools.

Gombrich wrote with British traditions in mind, but clearly the situation in the United States is worse, as anyone realizes who has taught in
higher education in recent decades. Yet students should not be blamed
personally for knowing so little about their cultural heritage; rather, the
fault rests with the social, cultural, and political currents of the time,
which have stressed other goals. One ultimate consequence of severing
the present from the past, however, will be the death of the humanities whose very reason for being is the maintenance of continuity with
traditions of culture. "To cut them off from these traditions," writes
Gombrich, "is to kill them."[4] What makes the situation in intellectual
life so alarming is that fewer and fewer scholars share Gombrich's concern about the possible fate of the humanities. Rather, what we are wit-
nessing is something like the systematic dismantling of the study of the
traditional humanities. In 1961 Gombrich could not have imagined the
intensity of the attack launched on the Western cultural heritage for
its alleged inherent oppressiveness—charges that, in view of the great
human monuments this tradition has produced, numb the mind. This
book, however, instead of contributing to the denigration of Western
beliefs and values, will inquire into ways to preserve and convey them.

But consider now the task of the educational evaluator, who might be asked to assess a program for teaching general knowledge, the contents of which have been characterized as hazy, vague, superficial, and consisting in many instances of little more than myth. Whatever happened to the idea of the emancipation of thought from myth? Gombrich's answer (and later Hirsch's answer) is that general knowledge, although often imprecise and lacking in detail, makes the mind feel at home on the map of culture. (I take special note of this cartographical image because I will avail myself of it in chapter 6, where I discuss curriculum as itinerary and teaching as the preparation of percipient art world sojourners.) The problem concerns how to make the young feel at home on the map of culture when their awareness is being extended well beyond the bounds of Western civilization (see chapter 5).

To provide some perspective on the need to restore general knowledge, Gombrich takes a leaf from established religion, which has a large and successful record of orienting its members to its doctrines. He suggests that culture needs both a creed and a catechism. What is more, we must first know the creed before we can criticize it. Secular equivalents of Isidore of Seville are needed who will commit themselves to identifying the knowledge deemed indispensable. Gombrich believes that any such cultural creed must be given a strong historical dimension, for that is conspicuously absent today. This creed should be encapsulated into a document that could be read and learned in an afternoon, which would make it longer than the Lord's Prayer, the Pledge of Allegiance, the Twenty-third Psalm, or, for that matter, the general orders that military inductees must memorize. But the document should be long enough, and the creed sufficiently intriguing, to stimulate young minds to inquiry. Gombrich also wonders about the prospects for convening a contemporary version of the Council of Nicaea, which would invite representatives of various cultures to present their own credos for mutual enlightenment and edification. Here, as one example, is Gombrich's sketch of a creed of Western civilization:

> I belong to Western Civilization, born in Greece in the first millennium B.C. It was created by poets, philosophers, artists, historians and scientists who freely examined the earlier myths and traditions of the ancient Orient. It flourished in Athens in the fifth century, was carried East by Macedonian conquests in the fourth century and in the first by Latin-speaking Romans to large parts of Europe and North Africa.

It was transformed by Christianity, which arose among the Jews of Palestine and spread throughout the Latin- and Greek-speaking world in the second and third centuries A.D. It survived the collapse of the Roman Empire under the pressure of Teutonic tribes in the fifth century, for the Greek and Roman Churches preserved some of its organization, its literature and its art during the so-called Middle Ages, when most of the barons and their serfs were illiterate. It began to flourish once more in the twelfth and thirteenth centuries when the Gothic style of building spread from France over Europe and when the growing universities of France, Italy and England gained fresh knowledge of Greek science and learning through translations made by Mohammedan Arabs, who had penetrated through North Africa to Spain. These also brought Arabic numerals from India, and paper, gun powder and the marine compass from China, thus assisting the emancipation of the merchant cities of fourteenth- and fifteenth-century Italy, which encouraged the recovery of Greek and Roman literature, art and building styles that is called the Renaissance. Its New Learning was disseminated by the printing press, which inaugurated the Modern Age and prepared the ground for the Reformation that split Europe in the sixteenth century, while voyages of discovery led to Portuguese, Spanish and English conquests and settlements across the seas.

It was transformed once more at that time by the renewed faith in the progress of human knowledge, exemplified in the mathematical theories of experimental science created in Italy and developed in the seventeenth-century Netherlands and Protestant English whence, in the eighteenth century, ideals of rationalism and tolerance spread to the Continent. It was thus enabled to survive the rapid increase in population that favored the Industrial Revolution, which led to nineteenth-century colonialism, the spread of literacy and the mass movements of socialism and nationalism. It endangered and transformed, in our century, most other cultures of the globe, which has shrunk for us to sputnik size by the invention of flying. I hope there will be a twenty-first century. Amen. (22–23)

CHAPTER TWO

Hirsch on
Cultural Literacy

COMING ACROSS Gombrich's essay, which was published almost thirty years before E. D. Hirsch's analysis of our educational problems and his recommendations for improving American schooling, one is tempted to say, "But that's just what Hirsch is saying!" Well, not exactly, but one is struck by the similarity of concern and commentary. The differences between the two writers are, of course, apparent: One is a European art historian who sought refuge from persecution and is addressing the situation in higher education in England; the other is an American literary theorist who has strong roots in this country's cultural heritage and is trying to improve teaching and learning in the schools. Gombrich nonetheless provides a context that helps to understand Hirsch's effort. As a preface to a more detailed discussion of Hirsch's ideas, it might be helpful to indicate how I became interested in Hirsch's writing.

I responded favorably to Hirsch's discussion of cultural literacy for several reasons. First, I had been thinking along similar lines, having long questioned theories of arts education that stress what Hirsch calls the content-neutral teaching of skills and abilities. Second, in a graduate course that I have taught for more than twenty years I have observed, especially during the eighties, a notable shrinkage in the amount of general knowledge that students bring to the course. The course, which addresses problems in justifying and teaching the arts in the schools, presupposes no more than commonplace knowledge about the arts. This is because I simply cannot rely on whether teachers' college graduates in fields outside the arts have had any substantive work in the arts; even arts education specialists who possess technical skills are often severely deficient in historical and cultural knowledge. For example, in one class, the only student who could identify the second movement of Beethoven's Third Symphony was from the People's Republic of China. Not only that, but she could also give an analysis of it. What is more, it is not uncommon for students to have had more coursework in non-Western than in Western art. My point is not to criticize American students for not having minimal cultural knowledge, but rather to underline a problem in our culture and educational system.

A third reason for my interest in Hirsch's thesis was that I had become familiar over the years with the work of Harry S. Broudy, an esteemed colleague whose rationale for general education in the schools places great importance on the role of tacit, contextual knowledge in interpreting and understanding new material. Indeed, his test for cultural literacy is the same as Hirsch's—the intelligent reading of a newspaper. What is more, as a faculty member of the College of Education at the University of Illinois at Urbana-Champaign, I was aware of the research on reading being conducted at the university's renowned Center for the Study of Reading, whose important work Hirsch acknowledges.

Fourth, I have long been preoccupied with the idea of culture and the problems of defining cultural and educational relations. I was intrigued, for example, by the debate that ensued from the publication in 1959 of C. P. Snow's *The Two Cultures and the Scientific Revolution*, which analyzed the relations between humanistic and scientific cultures.[1] Hirsch's *Cultural Literacy*, which contains a list of five thousand names, phrases, dates, and concepts that all Americans should know, presents yet another slant on the two-cultures discussion, this time with an emphasis on cultural literacy as opposed to cultural illiteracy and an urgent plea to abolish the latter. The scientific terms on Hirsch's word list in the book, supplied by his colleague James Trefil, constitute not what literate Americans actually know, but what they *should* know about science. This part of the list is thus prescriptive, whereas the rest is intended to be descriptive. Finally, owing to an interest in aesthetics and literary theory, I was familiar with Hirsch's theoretical writing and have followed with interest the debate over the role of intention in evaluating works of art in which he is a key discussant.

I noticed Hirsch's conversion to the importance of content-specific methods of teaching reading and writing (for he previously had been committed to a principles or skills approach to the teaching of reading) while I was writing *Excellence in Art Education*, which was undertaken at the invitation of the National Art Education Association and constitutes a response to the excellence-in-education movement of the 1980s.[2] Hirsch's *American Scholar* article, written before his *Cultural Literacy*, confirmed for me what I had been saying about the tendencies of writers in the field of arts education to stress procedure over substance.[3] *Excellence in Art Education* singled out what was in fact one of the more substantive reports in arts education to come out in the eighties, a report that nonetheless settled for teaching ways of knowing rather than specific content.[4] Typical of so many discussions of arts education, the report's basic weakness was its ritualistic obeisance to "alternatives," a deference that reflects a critical indecisiveness and contributes to the fragmentation of arts education. Any serious study of the arts will entertain alternatives, but that must occur within a framework that rejects an injudicious pluralism.

For these reasons, my interpretation of excellence in arts education stressed both procedural and substantive considerations. It emphasized the importance of building a sense of art in the young at a time when the nature and function of art have become problematic and the field of arts education is in need of wise guidance. A sense of art is important because it enables people to realize the benefits that works of art at their best are capable of providing. As an educational objective, I said the building of a sense of art can be best attained through a humanities-based curriculum that features creative, historical, and cultural studies and extends through all the years of schooling. But I left things neither to chance nor a plethora of alternatives. Instead, I recommended a specific curriculum, especially for the secondary years, which provides opportunities for comparative studies and yet concentrates on the masterworks of the Western cultural heritage. In subsequent writings I have elaborated this position to accommodate the elementary years as well (chapter 6).

Overall, the excellence-in-education literature of the 1980s was more balanced in its recommendations for educational reform than was the structure-of-subjects literature of the 1960s, which in large was inspired by Jerome S. Bruner's *The Process of Education*.[5] Except for some educational theorists' speculations about what the teaching of art as a subject might consist of and a token program supported by the government, reformers were principally concerned with mathematics and the sciences.

In the eighties, on the other hand, in books such as John Goodlad's *A Place Called School*, Ernest Boyer's *High School*, Mortimer Adler's *The Paideia Proposal*, and Theodore Sizer's *Horace's Compromise*, the study of the arts was assigned a significant place.[6] In the nineties, the pendulum is swinging back again toward an emphasis on mathematics and the sciences, not out of fear of Russian advances in space technology, as was the case in the sixties, but because of economic competition from other nations.

Now those who have been around for awhile might find it easy to shrug off yet more talk about reform. Since midcentury, wave after wave of reform proposals have washed over the educational landscape, and it is a moot question whether they have resulted in important educational gains or in the further erosion of the quality of learning. It seems likely that the current reform moves will be no more successful than previous ones. But whatever the effort and rhetoric of the moment, we cannot ignore questions about the role of the arts and humanities, for it is only through the study of the arts and humanities (in the traditional senses of these terms, the fine arts, literature, history, philosophy, and religion) that the quest for human significance can be pursued meaningfully.

While I was writing *Excellence in Art Education*, I realized that the interest in excellence would quickly crest. But this did not matter, for my recommendations were not only for the present but also for the year 2000 and beyond. It is the same for Hirsch's recommendations for the development of cultural literacy. The simple, basic fact remains that the slippage in minimal cultural literacy is alarming and adversely affects the quality of life. We are once again reminded that Matthew Arnold was right when he predicted in the nineteenth century that modern democracies would experience difficulties if they failed to sustain their preoccupation with the quality of life and learning.

One of the most surprising things about *Cultural Literacy* is that it became a best-seller, for Hirsch's voice is quiet and scholarly and his criticism restrained. Most readers probably found his discussion of technical research on reading as abstract as Allan Bloom's discussion of French philosophers in *The Closing of the American Mind*.[7] Descriptions of schema research, which are central to Hirsch's argument, lack intrinsic interest for anyone but specialists. The concurrent appearance of Hirsch's *Cultural Literacy* and Bloom's volume, with its dramatic subtitle (*How Higher Education Has Failed Democracy and Impoverished the Souls of Today's Students*), however, was probably responsible for much of the publicity that Hirsch's book received. But there was more to it than that. Just as C. P. Snow's discussion of the two cultures had touched a sensitive nerve in many readers, so Bloom's and Hirsch's writings gave voice to a widespread apprehension: Something seemed to be very wrong in American higher education and in our public schools, and the time had arrived to do something about it. On the surface at least, it seemed that Hirsch was providing a remedy to the crisis Bloom described. Whether or not one agrees with the arguments of the authors, this seems to explain the reception of the two books, which are otherwise quite different and should not have been reviewed together.

Hirsch's ideas about cultural literacy date from the late 1970s and achieved recognition with his *American Scholar* article in 1983.[8] Here we find the repudiation of his previous belief that specific content was less important in teaching reading comprehension than a learner's grasp of underlying psycholinguistic principles. In light of research conducted by himself and others, Hirsch gradually became convinced that "the content-indifferent, how-to approach to literacy skills is enormously oversimplified" (164). He termed reliance on this approach "romantic educational formalism," a view of pedagogy that fails to account for the fact that effective reading "involves both 'linguistic-schemata' (systems of expectation) and 'content-schemata' as well" (165). Among the several examples Hirsch cites to illustrate the significance of schema research, perhaps the most dramatic was his discovery that seventeen- and eighteen-year-olds in Richmond, Virginia, had difficulty reading passages about the Civil War because they did not know the names *Grant* and *Lee*. Yet without some acquaintance with these names, the mastery of reading skills (for example, sentence structure, parallelism, unity, focus, and so forth) is of little assistance. In other words, without a body of shared general knowledge, effective comprehension and communication become highly attenuated.

  In the *American Scholar* article Hirsch calls shared background knowledge "canonical knowledge," by which he means "the translinguistic knowledge on which linguistic literacy depends" (165). In later writing, however, he avoids the use of "canonical," probably because he realized that his readers would tend to associate canonical knowledge with a canon of works that all should study. But Hirsch does not advocate the study of a canon of works:

Acculturation into a national literate culture might be defined as learning what the "common reader" of a newspaper in a literate culture could be expected to know. That would include knowledge of certain values (whether or not one accepted them), and knowledge of such things as (for example) the First Amendment, Grant and Lee, and DNA. In our own culture, what should these contents be? Surely one answer to that should *partly* define our school curriculum. Acculturation into a literate culture (the *minimal aim* of schooling; we should still aim higher) could be defined as the gaining of cultural literacy. (166, emphasis added)

What is noteworthy about Hirsch's definition of cultural literacy is what so many of his critics overlooked: Cultural literacy consists of a knowledge of values as well as facts, and developing it constitutes only a minimal aim of schooling. Schools need to do much more. In these respects the proposals of "Cultural Literacy" are quite modest. Hirsch goes on to emphasize that general background information is not static, but inevitably changes. Much of it is acquired implicitly and informally, "through the pores" as it were, and also—a characteristic of cultural literacy that Hirsch's critics were to pounce upon—general information is both vague and superficial. For example, persons do not need much information about DNA or the First Amendment in order to comprehend newspaper discussions about these topics; in most situations, a little knowledge goes far enough. For those seeking further information, there are places where they can find it. The task for curriculum designers is to decide on the minimal cultural literacy needed for getting along in society and which items ought to be studied in greater detail. Decisions about the latter allow for greater flexibility and more opportunities for local choice and alternatives. Most of all, Hirsch pleads for a middle way between educational formalism and excessive pluralism, a way that will unite the various fragments of a literate culture. "Cultural Literacy" and Hirsch's subsequent writings present just such a middle way.

The remainder of the article discusses ways of forging a national consensus about the contents of cultural literacy, with the full realization that given our system of local school control, influence can be achieved only through persuasion. Developing cultural literacy, moreover, involves more than the mechanical teaching of a word list. Proper names, dates, phrases, and concepts, many of which symbolize or embody values, function "as a guide to objects of instruction" (168). It would be foolish, for example, to teach that the Fifth Amendment is one of ten amendments to the Constitution that make up the Bill of Rights without further contextualizing such information and making it interesting to learners.

Hirsch concludes by arguing that if he is right in his interpretation of the evidence, "We can only raise our reading and writing skills significantly by consciously redefining and extending our cultural literacy. And yet our current national effort in the schools is largely run on the premise that the best way to proceed is through a culturally neutral, skills-approach to reading and writing" (169).

I have started with Hirsch's *American Scholar* article because it sets out briefly and concisely the background and gist of his thesis. And it was because I had read the article and appreciated its point and sound sense that I was pleased when Hirsch accepted my invitation to write the lead article for a special issue of the *Journal of Aesthetic Education*, which I edit, devoted to the topic "Cultural Literacy and Arts Education." That issue was the first product of the research project under discussion and has since been published in book form (discussed in chapter 4).

Given my reasons for responding positively to Hirsch's concern and recommendations, I would like to think that my colleagues in the field of arts education would recognize the need to give greater attention to the specific content that should be studied. Yet despite recent efforts to complement creative and performing activities in arts classes with historical and critical studies, the field of arts education continues to be dominated by process theories and methodologies. Even an approach to arts education that has grown out of the cognitive revolution in understanding human behavior tends, for all its impressive theoretical underpinning, to favor the teaching of ways of thinking at the expense of specific content. Thus, following a period when the image of the child as artist was under a cloud for presenting a misleading conception of aesthetic learning, that image is now being revived. The new cognitivists in arts education, predominantly developmental psychologists, talk far more about the importance of the child's thinking as it expresses itself in the material of an artistic medium than they do, for example, about the transmission of a common cultural heritage. Even when perceiving and judging artworks are the topics, the emphasis is on these acts themselves and not on the specific works that should elicit the responses of learners. Interest in a background of common information is largely absent.[9] The humanities-based interpretation of arts education to be discussed in chapter 6 offers an alternative to such process-based theories of arts education.

Cultural Literacy expresses three of Hirsch's basic concerns.[10] The first is with the impediments to the acculturation of the young posed by the unacceptably high rate of cultural illiteracy in society. The book's second concern is with the increasing fragmentation within society and its potential for divisiveness and social disorder. And the third concern is with the decline of America's ability to compete economically with other advanced nations. Cultural pluralism, the complexities of modern life, and romantic educational formalism are identified as the causes of cultural illiteracy, social conflict, and national decline. The development of cultural literacy is offered as at least a partial remedy for our educational problems and social ills. Such development consists of conveying minimal background knowledge acquired in what Hirsch calls an extensive curriculum (for students younger than thirteen), the application of schema theory research to building in the young the relevant cognitive maps needed for understanding and communicating, and the rededication of Americans to America's civil religion as it is articulated in Gunnar Myrdal's *An American Dilemma*, a classic study that played a major role in the development of Hirsch's thinking.[11]

In an updated and expanded edition of *Cultural Literacy* printed in 1988, Hirsch notes that in addition to typographical corrections and an improvement in the gloss on "Waltzing Matilda," the only major change necessary was a net increase of 343 items to the book's word list, items culled from about three thousand suggestions that the authors received in response to the first printing, bringing the total number of items on the list to five thousand. Only twenty-five items were deleted. Hirsch reiterates what he said in the *American Scholar* article: The development of cultural literacy does not encompass all of schooling; rather, it "focuses sharply on the background knowledge necessary for functional literacy and effective national communication" (xi). He further underlines the conservatism of literate culture. Although it is not completely static, the stock of general knowledge changes slowly; new elements are admitted only gradually. The influence of the women's movement and multiculturalism, cases in point, are reflected in the list. Yet Hirsch emphasizes that 80 percent of the words on the list have been in use for more than a hundred years. This is not surprising; without considerable continuity in the composition of cultural literacy, communication among individuals would be almost impossible. In short, "the goals of political liberalism require educational conservatism. We make social and economic progress *only* by teaching myths and facts that are predominantly traditional" (xii).

In the Preface of the book, Hirsch sets the stage and tone for what will follow: "To be culturally literate is to possess the basic information needed to thrive in the modern world" (xiii). Because this information spans the universes of human discourse and social classes, and although all persons require it, disadvantaged children in particular will suffer from a lack of it. Yet cultural literacy is declining among all ethnic groups and social classes, not just among minority groups. Hirsch also points out the mistake of those critics who assumed that the core knowledge he advocates would require all students to read a canon of great books. He further stresses the descriptive character of the list; except for the items on science, it is comprised of items that people who qualify as literate actually do know but may not always value. With the literate person as exemplar, however, the list does become prescriptive for the teaching of cultural literacy. Hirsch is attempting to clear up the misunderstanding that "canonical information" is not the same as "a canon." What is canonical is merely a certain level of literate performance.

The teaching of core knowledge is limited to what Hirsch calls the "extensive curriculum," that for approximately 50 percent of the elementary years, or for students roughly up to age thirteen. In addition to the extensive curriculum, there is the intensive curriculum, whose study is reserved for the secondary years, when matters can be studied in depth and greater flexibility and choice are possible. Again, it is fair to say that most of Hirsch's critics have either overlooked the distinction between the extensive curriculum and the intensive curriculum or willfully ignored it, with consequent distortion of his argument (see chapter 3).

The remainder of the Preface states Hirsch's belief that the causes of declining rates of literacy can be found in the eighteenth-century writings of Jean Jacques Rousseau and the modern influence of John Dewey. Citing *Schools of Tomorrow*, Hirsch claims that Dewey underestimated the importance of accumulating information and overestimated the value of studying only typical situations to which the problem solving method could be applied. But "only by piling up specific, communally shared information can children learn to participate in complex cooperative activities with other members of their community" (xv).

Hirsch is here simply appealing to an elementary insight of anthropology—all human communities acculturate their young by transmitting to them specific information shared by the adults in the society. The conviction that the young should try to grasp information held common among adults, even while they may still be too young to understand it fully, has naturally raised the eyebrows of developmental psychologists; yet there is something to the belief that even a partial understanding of a concept is better than no understanding. Not one to underestimate the uses of repetition, Hirsch observes that "only by accumulating shared symbols, and the shared information that the symbols represent, can we learn to communicate effectively with one another in our national community" (xvii). The proposition sounds commonsensical enough, and it is difficult to account for the storm of controversy it aroused. I have personally caused some dismay among friends and colleagues by taking Hirsch seriously. But then, many of those who have been quick to censure Hirsch often indicate by their remarks that they have not read his work carefully.

Hirsch begins with definitions of key terms. By "cultural literacy" he means what reading specialists call "world knowledge," that is, "the network of information that all competent readers possess. It is the background information, stored in their minds, that enables them to take up a newspaper and read it with an adequate level of comprehension, getting the point, grasping the implications, relating what they read to the unstated context which alone gives meaning to what they read" (2). Hirsch believes that educators have largely neglected this domain of background information and failed to appreciate the uses of superficial comprehension.

Core knowledge is characterized not only by a certain vagueness but also by a national, as opposed to a merely local, scope and a fair amount of stability. Culturally literate people may not have detailed insight into what they read, but they are capable of getting the drift, gist, or general shape of things. They can contextualize information, make relevant associations, and comprehend things at a certain level. In saying that cultural literacy has a national character, Hirsch is emphasizing that some things belong to it but not others—Abraham Lincoln and even Benedict Arnold, for example, but not Jeb Stuart. Yet, although core knowledge should be more than commonplace information (for example, that Lincoln was president during the Civil War and helped preserve the Union), it does not, to repeat, have to be detailed to be functional. As Hirsch puts the matter: "Cultural literacy lies *above* the everyday levels of knowledge that everyone possesses and *below* the expert level known only to specialists. It is that middle ground of cultural knowledge possessed by the 'common reader.' It includes information that we have traditionally expected our children to receive in school, but which they no longer do" (19).

Cultural literacy may further be understood in terms of its core and periphery. As indicated, the core, roughly 80 percent of the words on Hirsch's list, has been in use for a long time, whereas the periphery consists of those items that are subject to change. But this does not mean that the development of cultural literacy induces a conservative attitude. Among the contents of cultural literacy are ideas and concepts that can be used in talking about any viewpoint, including those of which one is critical. But people must first understand their culture before earning the right to judge it. Hirsch's convincing example in this regard (which his critics conveniently overlook) is the way that writers for the *Black Panther* presupposed the traditional core of the literate culture in advancing their grievances.

Cultural literacy is simply a necessity of anyone—conservative or liberal, reactionary or radical—who wishes to communicate effectively with others. It "has become the common currency for social and economic exchange . . . and the only available ticket to full citizenship" (22). Certainly, Congressman Major Owens, an African American, was assuming that he would be understood when he said in testimony against the nomination of Clarence Thomas to the Supreme Court that the reaction in the black community could be compared to that of the French and Norwegian people, respectively, if "the collaborative Marshall Pétain had been awarded a medal after World War II, or if in Norway Quisling had been made a high official in the government." [12]

This is precisely Hirsch's point. Such remarks are relatively meaningless to people who do not know the associations with *collaborator* and *quisling*, which have become part of the common currency of language since World War II. Whether one agrees or disagrees with Owens's views is less important than the fact that he assumed his constituents would understand his statements (*Quisling*, incidentally, is on Hirsch's word list). In this respect, literate culture is inherently democratic; it cuts across generations, social groups, gender lines, races, and classes and exists beyond the narrow spheres of family, neighborhood, and region.

In response to the criticism that the contents of cultural literacy are excessively Eurocentric, Hirsch reminds readers that his list does in fact accommodate the changing character and composition of American life. But because the mastery of the standard language of a literate society (in the case of the United States this would be the English language) is prerequisite to participating in its standard culture, Hirsch states emphatically that multiculturalism should not be the primary goal of American education. Although teaching an understanding of different cultures is important for inculcating tolerance and providing alternative perspectives, it should not supplant the schools' principal obligation to teach the mastery of American literate culture.

Such mastery was precisely what Malcolm X accomplished by reading the prison dictionary during the period of his incarceration. Jeff Smith, commenting on how Hirsch has been misunderstood, points out how, for Malcolm X, the acquisition of this knowledge included more than mere vocabulary memorization: "With every succeeding page," wrote Malcolm, "I also learned of people and places and events from history. Actually, the dictionary is like a miniature encyclopedia."[13] He also admits that before studying the dictionary he was not only inarticulate but also functionally ineffective. Malcolm X's experience shows that Hirsch's dictionary, far from marginalizing minority students and indoctrinating them in conservative viewpoints on culture and politics, could have the effect described by Malcolm X: the development of cultural literacy needed to communicate ideas. Smith remarks that "what's most interesting is that in telling his story, Malcolm X gives as much credit to Herodotus, H. G. Wells, Will Durant, and Arnold Toynbee as to minority writers like Ghandi, W. E. B. Du Bois, and Frederick Olmstead. He appears to have found all these writers inspiring. For all, including the privileged whites, helped him learn, and thus played a role in shaping his radical views."[14]

Because Hirsch's views are often termed sexist as well as elitist and racist, it is also worth pointing out that they are compatible with certain feminist perspectives on tradition and a common culture. Elizabeth Fox-Genovese, a feminist and the director of women's studies at Emory University, calls it an error to oppose a feminist view of tradition to a male version and writes that "a Hawaiian quilt or a Scottish ballad may embody the same human value as the *Mona Lisa*, but aesthetic value has its own claims, which concern for human equality and personal experience do not exhaust." Not only that. "The extreme claims of feminism point toward a radical personalization that risks undermining any aspiration to common standards and a common culture, including a common ideal of justice." [15] In other words, Fox-Genovese's espousal of feminism rests on other grounds. Given the examples I have cited, I think it fair to conclude that these beliefs are consistent with Hirsch's assertion that young people will enter neither a tribal society nor a global, transnational culture but a national literate culture.

The rest of Hirsch's discussions of the decline of cultural literacy refers to anecdotal and empirical evidence that documents the serious gaps in the general knowledge of young people and to the consequent need to rediscover the "great hidden problem of American education" — the importance of contextual information in understanding and communicating with others. Once more, it is essential that cultural literacy be cultivated in the early years; fifth grade may be too late, and tenth grade certainly is. Hirsch also has a few good words to say about memorization, reminding readers that cultures typically transmit their national languages to the young through repetitious drill. Children, moreover, are not averse to piling up information and making themselves expert about things that interest them.

The technical research that supports Hirsch's recommendations has provided a better understanding of the underlying processes of reading in that sense of reading that encompasses both reading and writing. Although "the discovery of the schema" came as no surprise to many of his readers, Hirsch is probably right in saying that educators have been slow to realize its pedagogical implications. Schema research "should induce a deep skepticism toward the belief that our schools can teach reading, writing, and critical thinking as all-purpose general skills applicable to novel problems," for "all cognitive skills depend on procedural and substantive schemata that are highly specific to the task at hand" (60–61). Nonetheless, the assertion of the inefficacy of general skills sounds counterintuitive and is arguable. Certain proponents of the teaching of critical thinking would certainly find it so. General skills would seem to have some applicability in a number of different contexts, but there is also an important truth in the research Hirsch cites. Levels of reading comprehension are closely associated with the amount of specific information a reader brings to reading, information without which technical reading skills are of little help.[16] What then is our current understanding of reading comprehension?

Effective reading involves an active mind that has the capacity not only to decode what is written down but also to supply contextual information for making sense of it. This information is part of the essential meaning of the text. According to Hirsch, "The explicit meanings of a piece of writing are the tip of the iceberg of meaning; the larger part lies below the surface of the text and is composed of the reader's own relevant knowledge. The past two decades of research have shown that such background knowledge is a far more important ingredient in the meaning process than earlier theoretical accounts had supposed" (34).

Central to understanding, reading comprehension is a picture of how the mind functions while making sense of things. Memory, of course, is crucial; it consists of long-term memory (the way most people think about memory) and short-term memory, which has difficulty holding on to more than four to seven separate items at a time. Any more would impede the effective performance of tasks. A device that improves the accomplishment of memory tasks is the "chunking" of information in the way, for example, that telephone and social security numbers are broken up for easier recall. Chunking is effective because it permits the application of both long-term and short-term memory capacities. As Hirsch puts it:

> Short-term memory is the mind's vestibule where incoming items enjoy a brief equality lasting just long enough for the mind to give them a structure. Short-term memory holds in momentary suspension items that have come in one after another, thus enabling us to convert them into a stable structure. Amidst the temporal flow of language, short-term memory allows us to form a few words into nontemporal structures. Then we transfer those structures to long-term memory, leaving short-term memory free to deal again with the temporal flow of incoming words. (35)

But, asks Hirsch, if short-term memory can hold items for only a very short time, how is it that we are capable of remembering so much, sometimes the meanings of whole books and conversations? Intuition suggests that we do it by recalling the essence of things, and this is precisely what happens. "Language is transferred from short-term memory into long-term memory not as a literal recollection of words but as a shorthand recoding of their gist, which normally erases from memory many of the individual words" (36). Another way of putting the matter is to say that surface features are quickly forgotten, but essential form is retained in memory. First comes "our initial understanding of a text [which] depends on our applying relevant background knowledge that is not given in the text itself" (38). Then, and this is the most important point, "We construct an elaborated model of what the words [of a text] *imply* and store that" (38–39). The fuller version of the text's meaning gets stored in long-term memory. Does this mean that background knowledge is part of the meaning of a text? The answer is yes; "Inferences based on prior knowledge are part of the meaning from the very beginning" (39). This view of sense-making, moreover, holds for interpreting visual images, not only verbal texts. Hirsch provides many telling examples to illustrate the functioning of mind in understanding and communicating.

Hirsch's discussion of the psychological structure of background knowledge explains the ways people interpret experience through typical exemplars or prototypes of basic category words. For example, the prototype of a bird, at least in this country, is one that has robinlike features. Although the term *prototype* is often used to refer to these basic categories, Hirsch, following Richard Anderson, prefers the term *schema* (plural *schemata*). Synonyms for schemata are *frames, concepts, models, scripts, lenses,* and so forth. Of course, cultural literacy depends on the possession of concepts that go considerably beyond such basic-level terms as *tree, bird,* and *dog.* To reiterate: "A schema functions as a unified system of background relationships whose visible parts stand for the rest of the schema." And "schemata are our necessary instruments for making the surfaces of what we read connect significantly with the background knowledge that is withheld from immediate consciousness by the limits of short-term memory" (54–55).

Also critical to reading comprehension—and to interpreting visual and auditory images—is a group of primary associations that are shared within a culture. Because Hirsch thinks that proponents of content-indifferent methods of teaching skills have overlooked the importance of specific background information, he prefers to discuss "skill as knowledge and knowledge as skill" in order to emphasize "the knowledge-bound character of *all* cognitive skills. All cognitive skills," he writes, "depend on procedural and substantive schemata that are highly specific to the task at hand" (60–61). Or, "People do not develop general, transferable skills in problem solving, critical thinking, or in any other field" (62). At this point, Hirsch provides an illuminating analogy of skill in reading to skill in playing chess.

> Skill in reading is like skill in chess in many respects. Good reading, like good chess, requires the rapid deployment of schemata

that have already been acquired and do not have to be worked out on the spot. Good readers, like good chess players, quickly recognize typical patterns, and, since they can ignore many small-scale features of the text, they have space in short-term memory to take in an overall structure of meaning. They are able to do all of this because, like expert chess players, they have ready access to a large number of relevant schemata. By contrast, unskilled readers lack this large store of relevant schemata and must therefore work out many small-scale meaning relationships while they are reading. These demanding tasks quickly overload their short-term memories, making their performance slow, arduous, and ineffective. (63)

Now, we tend to be indifferent to the ideas of writers when they merely confirm what we have taken for granted, for example, that our ability to make sense of what we read, see, and hear is a function of our contextualizing powers. But when such research casts serious doubt on unquestioned assumptions, then it deserves more attention.

In an interesting chapter devoted to showing the connections between the development of a national language and a national culture, Hirsch indicates that historical research reinforces psychological investigations. He explains how education helps to keep national languages stable through standards embodied in dictionaries, spelling books, and various other kinds of texts. The emergence of national languages in the modern era, moreover, can be understood in light of the need of industrial societies to establish a common and stable means of communication among persons and groups with diverse, specialized interests. The stability of written national languages codified by deliberate political and educational decisions contrasts with the relative instability of oral traditions of communication that tend to be characterized by constant change.

Hirsch had remarked that the contents of cultural literacy consist of more than commonplace knowledge but less than expert knowledge. He also distinguishes three domains of a national language: an international domain, which encompasses certain items that people anywhere in the world should know; a transcultural domain, which defines the basic need for literacy in English wherever English is spoken; and a national domain, which contains knowledge specific to one's own country. All national cultures develop dictionaries, textbooks, and other materials that contain their respective vocabularies, and those that fail to do so find it difficult to evolve into modern states. China, observes Hirsch, is one example, primarily because of the major differences between written and spoken Chinese. The discussion of the evolution of national dictionaries helps to explain Hirsch's interest in publishing dictionaries of cultural literacy.

Particularly noteworthy are the ways national languages transcend those of particular regions, groups, and social classes. Because they are more encompassing, compendiums of cultural literacy can help outsiders enter mainstream culture and thus produce progressive, liberalizing, and democratizing effects. No one needs to feel left out. But such desirable results are possible only if we recognize the importance of general information—precisely what schools fail to do. Just as Hirsch argued against multiculturalism as a primary educational priority, so he cautions against imposing multilingualism on students before they have achieved monoliteracy in a national language. We tempt social fragmentation, civil antagonism, cultural illiteracy, and technological and economic decline if we forget that a monoliterate language and culture must come first. In this connection, Hirsch distinguishes Jeffersonian pluralism from linguistic pluralism; the former encourages diversity of traditions, values, and opinions but not at the expense of national language or national culture (further discussed in chapter 5).

Ultimately, however, what holds the American national culture together, in addition to the English language and legal codes, is a civil religion. What is a civil religion?

> Our civil ethos [writes Hirsch] treasures patriotism and loyalty as high, though perhaps not ultimate, ideals and fosters the belief that the conduct of the nation is guided by a vaguely defined God. Our tradition places importance on carrying out the rites and ceremonies of our civil ethos and religion through the national flag, the national holidays, and the national anthem (which means "national hymn"), and supports the morality of tolerance and benevolence, of the Golden Rule, and communal cooperation. We believe in altruism and self-help, in quality, freedom, truth telling, and respect for the national law. (98–99)

A nonsectarian religion, this civil religion is accepted by sectarians for the sake of the common good and domestic tranquility. The "bible" and the "books" of this religion are well known to literate Americans—the

Constitution, the Declaration of Independence, the Bill of Rights, and similar documents. The fundamental principles and values of a civil religion are the sovereignty of the individual, justice, freedom, and equality. Hirsch uses Martin Luther King's "I Have a Dream" speech to show how the values of America's civil religion are manifested and how they constitute the operative religion of the land.

But understanding the role that civil religion plays in a national culture does not answer completely the questions of the nature of a national vocabulary and the contents of a national culture. At this point Hirsch identifies three segments of an American public culture: the American civil religion and its peculiar traditions and values; the middle domain of culture proper with its politics, customs, technological idioms, legends, and so on; and the value-neutral vocabulary of national discourse that people use to discuss any aspect of life whatsoever. Although the lines between these segments are obviously not sharp, the middle segment, the domain of culture proper, is the most dynamic of the three because of its greater susceptibility to change. Arguments and debates about the contents of this domain also call for a flexible and accommodative vocabulary. But how does the vocabulary itself arise? Well, someone had to suggest what it is that we can no longer take for granted, and Hirsch, his colleagues, and the foundation he heads, have taken on this task. But before elaborating, Hirsch emphasizes that such a vocabulary is not elitist, racist, sexist, or exclusively ethnocentric.

In defense of his project, Hirsch points out that published vocabularies have historically neither fixed the national language nor reflected the coherent culture of a dominant class. This was shown by studies done in the large cities of Asia and Europe that detailed how newcomers to London, for example, influenced mainstream culture as much as they were influenced by it. Given the need for a common medium of discourse, the interplay of diverse dialects produced "a common, composite speech for use in public discourse," that is, "an amalgam that had no single identifiable parent" and "did not represent the speech of any particular location, class, or ethnic group" (105). If it appeared that cultural literacy was closely related to social class, it was because only groups that were sufficiently well off could afford the education that conveyed the vocabulary in question. But modern democracies are committed to universal schooling and the abolition of privileges that derive solely from wealth and social class. Indeed, the Jeffersonian ideal of citizenry implies a strong correlation between the development of a literate culture and democratic government. Consequently, writes Hirsch, it is "a very odd cliché that connects literate national culture with elitism, since it is the least elitist or exclusive culture that exists in any modern nation" (106). By contrast, ethnic, pop, or youth cultures are more exclusive because of their tendency to cultivate the values of in-groups and express generational or geographical preferences.

In response to the multilinguists' complaint that his lexicon of cultural literacy relies too heavily on the English language, Hirsch points out the obvious: English is simply the basic language of the American literate culture. That the prominence of English is due to accidents of history makes it no less a fact. No claim is made that the traditions of the English language are either superior or inferior; they just happen to be the traditions that Americans share. To deny some Americans the opportunities to become proficient in English is thus to deny them effective participation in national affairs. Cultural illiteracy is disenfranchising; cultural literacy is empowering. Without cultural literacy, people cannot judge matters of importance that concern them. Accordingly, Hirsch recalls the Ciceronian ideal of education and discourse: "Literacy—reading and writing taken in a serious sense—is the rhetoric of our day, the basis of public discourse in a modern republic. The teaching of Ciceronian literacy as our founders conceived it is a primary but currently neglected responsibility of our schools" (109).

When academic intellectuals address educational matters they often display indifference or hostility toward the educational establishment, its member educationists, and its standard literature. It is clear, however, that Hirsch has done some homework. His observations range over a number of studies, key documents, and philosophical writings about education. Although he is critical of what he calls educational formalism, the origins of which he ascribes to Rousseau and Dewey, his criticism avoids flamboyant rhetoric. In contrast to studies that play down the influence of schools and teachers on learning, he takes schools, teachers, and their obligations seriously.

But just what is the educational formalism Hirsch denounces? "Educational formalism assumes that the specific contents used to teach 'language arts' do not matter so long as they are closely tied to what the child already knows, but this developmental approach ignores . . . [the] important point that different children know different things. Current school books in language arts pay little systematic attention to conveying a body of culturally significant information from grade to grade" (112). In urging a compromise between the extremes of traditionalism and pragmatism, Hirsch recommends "a curriculum that is traditional in content but diverse in its emphases, that is pluralistic in its interests and modes of teaching, but nonetheless provides our children with a common core of cultural information" (126–27).

There are writers on education who have anticipated Hirsch's concern and a body of significant educational literature that, his homework notwithstanding, he does not discuss or acknowledge (discussed in chapter 6). But I am less interested in filling the lacunae in Hirsch's knowledge of educational literature than in pointing out his important recommendations for reform. A key distinction to understanding his proposals is that between an *extensive* curriculum, the domain proper of cultural literacy, and an *intensive* curriculum in which things are studied in greater depth and where more choice and flexibility are possible.

> One can think of the school curriculum as consisting of two complementary parts, which might be called the extensive curriculum and the intensive curriculum. The content of the extensive curriculum is traditional literate knowledge, the information, attitudes, and assumptions that literate Americans share—cultural literacy. Of course, this curriculum should be taught not just as a series of terms, or list of words, but as a *vivid system of shared associations*. The name John Brown should evoke in children's minds not just a simple identifying definition but a whole network of lively traits, the traditionally known facts and values. (127, emphasis added)

Beyond the extensive curriculum there is the intensive curriculum.

> The intensive curriculum, though different, is equally essential. Intensive study encourages a fully developed understanding of a subject, making one's knowledge of it integrated and coherent. It coincides with Dewey's recommendation that children should be deeply engaged with a small number of typical concrete instances. It is also that part of the total curriculum in which great flexibility in contents and methods can prevail. The intensive curriculum is the more pluralistic element of my proposal, because it ensures that individual students, teachers, and schools can work intensively

with materials that are appropriate for their diverse temperaments and aims. (128)

This two-part curriculum (extensive and intensive) is what many critics overlooked so completely that one wonders whether chapter 5 of Hirsch's book was read at all. Consequently, Hirsch's critics are mistaken when they say that he advocates the mandatory reading of a canon of works. There is a difference between core knowledge and a canon. Of course, there are certain writers, for example Shakespeare, whom Hirsch would want all students to study, but in the intensive curriculum there could be a choice of reading, say, *Romeo and Juliet, Julius Caesar, Hamlet,* and *Macbeth.*

Although Hirsch quite sensibly acknowledges that it may be necessary to learn a large number of things by rote and that accumulating a lot of information about something can be not only interesting but also useful, he does not think that either extensive or intensive information should be taught as mere catalogs, which his word list considered in isolation might suggest. Information needs to be contextualized and made interesting in order for young people to master it. Hirsch is thus not proposing that teachers' colleges prepare legions of Gradgrinds, but rather that they educate teachers who are culturally literate in Hirsch's sense and capable of adapting information to students' backgrounds and interests. The contents of cultural literacy should be integrated into lesson plans that are included in spellers, textbooks, dictionaries, and so on. Efforts should be made to establish linkages among systems of minimally shared meanings and associations—schemata linked to schemata linked to schemata. Teachers should always use contextual information in such a way that it will make a subject more accessible to students and not obscure or trivialize it. This is especially important in the teaching of the arts, for all too often artworks are rendered imperceptible by their enmeshment in a jumble of unrelated and unintelligible information.

We may agree with Hirsch that educational theorists, curriculum designers, and teachers need to take a long and scrutinizing look at a content-neutral skills approach to teaching not only reading and writing but also the teaching of all subjects, including the arts. A modest proposal then—only a few hundred pages, observes Hirsch, separates the culturally illiterate from the culturally literate—nonetheless turns out to be quite important. At stake, Hirsch argues, is nothing less than "breaking the cycle of illiteracy for deprived children; raising the living standard of families who have been illiterate; making our country more competitive in international markets; achieving greater social justice; enabling all citizens to participate in the political process; bringing us closer to the Ciceronian ideal of universal public discourse—in short, achieving fundamental goals of the Founders at the birth of the republic" (145).

CHAPTER THREE

The Reception of
Cultural Literacy

Hᵢᵣₛcₕ'ₛ ᵢᵈₑₐ of cultural literacy has been set out in some detail because his message has been largely misunderstood and in some instances willfully distorted and maligned. Many of his critics dismiss *Cultural Literacy* as nothing more than cultural trivia or an endorsement of mindless rote learning. Others, incredibly, perceive incipient fascism in it. Hirsch himself may be partly responsible for failing to communicate his ideas, and I will have more to say about this later. It is especially those critics located on the political far left who have gone out of their way to trivialize and demean his effort. Typically, they combine misinterpretation with crude invective. Because of the pervasiveness of this kind of writing—that is, the abandonment of disinterested reviewing in favor of the superimposition on a text of the reviewer's own ideological perspective—I will discuss one representative example: the review of *Cultural Literacy* by Stanley Aronowitz and Henry A. Giroux that was first published in the *Harvard Educational Review* and later reprinted in the authors' *Postmodern Education: Politics, Culture, and Social Criticism.*[1]

Aronowitz and Giroux open their discussion by declaring that it will consist of a critique of the right-wing views of not only Hirsch but also Allan Bloom. The books of these two writers, they argue,

> represent the logic of a new cultural offensive, one of the most elaborate conservative educational manifestos to appear in decades. But it is important to recognize that this offensive represents

a form of textual authority that not only legitimates a particular version of Western civilization as well as an elitist notion of the canon, but also serves to exclude all those other discourses, whether from the new social movements or from other sources of opposition, which attempt to establish different grounds for the production and organization of knowledge. In effect, the new cultural offensive is not to be understood simply as a right-wing argument for a particular version of Western civilization or as a defense for what is seen as a legitimate academic canon, both of these concerns have to be seen as part of a broader struggle over textual authority. In this case, the notion of textual authority is about the right-wing shift from the discourse of class to the broader relationship between knowledge and power, and the struggle to control the very grounds on which knowledge is produced and legitimated. What is at issue here is not simply how different discourses function to reference particular forms of intellectual, ethical, and social relations but how power works as both a medium and outcome of what we might call a form of textual politics. (26)

The authors' misreading of Hirsch's text is apparent from the very beginning. They say that he "attempts to enlist the language of culture and the culture of literacy as bases for rethinking the American past and reconstructing the discourse of public life." But Hirsch's concepts of culture and literacy perform no such tasks. Hirsch neither rethinks American history nor reconstructs the language of a literate culture. He simply attempts to identify what literate Americans already know and the vocabulary they use to understand and communicate with one another. Because of the way Hirsch has characterized cultural literacy—quite literally as the empowerment and enfranchisement of the culturally illiterate—it is absurd to say that he "is deeply committed to cleansing democracy of its critical and emancipatory possibilities" (38).

Nothing more is needed to affirm Hirsch's sentiments than a glance at his concluding remarks on page 145, which were quoted at the end of chapter 2. Hirsch wants to reinvigorate democracy by empowering the young, by giving them a higher level of literacy. He wants to raise the level of cultural literacy in order to increase participation in public discourse. If anything, a culturally literate citizenry will have the intellectual capacity to keep the powerful and the privileged in check and take them to task when necessary. Hirsch, moreover, is aware of the ambiguous relation of cultural knowledge to truth. Although much of the content of cultural literacy, as Hirsch sees it, is factual and true, much is also vague and hazy but important nonetheless.

Aronowitz and Giroux further falsify Hirsch when they say that he rejects pluralism in favor of cultural uniformity. As his word list shows, he appreciates the pluralistic origins of its terms. What he finds dangerously divisive, and ultimately dysfunctional, for newcomers to the culture as well as for young people who must learn to live in a society with numerous and implacable givens is an unfettered pluralism in which each group exacts strict obedience to its own language and values. It is true that Hirsch does not think that the schools should be an arena of political contention. He reasons that meaningful political struggle cannot be initiated unless contending parties have a firm grounding in the literacy of the culture being contested; such background knowledge is simply a precondition for any sort of debate, liberal or conservative, radical or reactionary. Acculturation must, therefore, come first. And far from understanding "cultural literacy" primarily in terms of artifacts or a canon of great books, Hirsch clearly takes it to be a power of mind, but one that young people are increasingly being denied the ability to develop and exercise. This is especially true for the young people of disadvantaged minorities.

Furthermore, that a national literate culture by definition holds certain important things in common does not imply that cultural literacy is solely a means for promoting social order and contentment. Dissatisfaction may demand change, but only culturally literate people have the capacity to modify social arrangements and humanize authority. We are reminded once more of the high stakes at issue in developing cultural literacy: not only a more competitive economy (a need for any modern society) but also, and even more important, the improved social equity and more widespread participation in political life that can be achieved when the yoke of cultural illiteracy is lifted from those who are now oppressed by it. Again, this is the Ciceronian ideal of universal public discourse endorsed by Jefferson and the other founders of the Republic.

Aronowitz and Giroux further mislead readers when they characterize the items on Hirsch's word list as unrelated categories of information but neglect to point out that Hirsch emphasizes the need to contextualize information in order to make it meaningful and interesting. Aronowitz and Giroux also begin to strain credibility when their rhetoric casts Hirsch as an "aristocratic traditionalist" who wants "to replace democratic educational authority" and asserts that he (along with Bloom) represents a "resurgent attempt on the part of right-wing intellectuals and ruling groups to undermine the bastions of democratic public life as we have known it over the past two decades" (39).

The association of Hirsch's ideas with the policies of the Reagan administration further weakens the writers' credibility when it is realized that Hirsch's recommendations for reform derive principally from reading research that has been conducted since the seventies. Moreover, Hirsch's liberal sentiments and commitments are evident throughout his text; it is merely name-calling to characterize the book as a version of "the conservative educational credo" (39). The remark falsely suggests that all conservatives subscribe to a single educational policy. The ploy used here is the familiar one that ascribes guilt through association.

There are still more distortions in Aronowitz and Giroux's review; for example, they ascribe to Hirsch a desire to impose the unifying facts, values, and writings of Western culture (Hirsch speaks of an American literate culture) on the schools, an act that Aronowitz and Giroux regard as an elitist power play that favors the winners in a society. Yet, elites would have much to fear from a culturally literate citizenry that has the ability to question their legitimacy. It is culturally literate citizens who put elites at risk and create opportunities for others to move into positions of authority. By constantly referring to Hirsch's word list as a set of unrelated *facts*, Aronowitz and Giroux fail to notice that many of the concepts imply *values* and must, for that reason alone if no other, be elaborated and contextualized to be understood properly.

Aronowitz and Giroux continue to misrepresent Hirsch with their claim that the contents of cultural literacy are fixed in the past. Although Hirsch acknowledges that cultural literacy is largely comprised of traditional, slow-changing items, it nonetheless constitutes a common linguistic currency that serves as the medium of exchange for any group— liberal, conservative, radical, reactionary, or the politically indifferent. Aronowitz and Giroux themselves must rely on such linguistic coin in order to communicate their own ideas.

Still another effort to drown Hirsch in a sea of epithets is the authors' contention that he is a determinist whose explanations are "simplistic" when, in fact, all Hirsch is claiming is a close relationship between the development of modern national states and national languages. Aronowitz and Giroux also speak of Hirsch's efforts to forge a "totalitarian unity," ignoring his endorsement of the local control of education and all the educational variety and departure from a centralized sources that it implies. To be sure, if Hirsch were saying that the extensive curriculum constitutes the whole of schooling and that the lexicon of cultural literacy is all that needs to be taught, the complaint would have some validity. But Aronowitz and Giroux completely omit reference to Hirsch's discussion of the intensive curriculum, where he provides for flexibility in the selection of both content and methods. Once more, the extensive curriculum occupies only 50 percent of the elementary years (for students under the age of thirteen) and is but one part of a two-part program. "Intensive curricular materials," on the other hand, which come into use during the secondary years of schooling, "can vary with circumstances and should depend on many grounds of choice, including student and teacher interest, local community preferences, and the aims and values that predominate in particular schools or classrooms." [2] Aronowitz and Giroux's silence on Hirsch's intensive curriculum is not surprising inasmuch as discussing it would have considerably weakened their critique.

In short, nothing in *Cultural Literacy* is acceptable to Aronowitz and Giroux. Hirsch's quite modest recommendations for educational reform are rejected as "highly dogmatic," "reactionary," "theoretically impoverished," "politically visionless," "incorrect," "repressive," "strangled by the past," and expressive of a "false egalitarianism," "ideological amnesia," "misplaced faith," "crippling ethnocentrism," and just about every other deadly sin. Poor Hirsch! All he wants to do is raise a little, perhaps by a few hundred pages' worth, the level of knowledge that all persons need to have to communicate and share information. Accordingly, one may ask whether it is the kind of critique produced by Aronowitz and Giroux that is dogmatic. Their intransigence has prompted two writers otherwise sympathetic to their views to comment on exponents on radical school reform. Gerald Graff and William E. Cain write that the difficulty with liberationist programs that writers such as Aronowitz and Giroux and their mentor, the Brazilian philosopher Paulo Freire, advance is that they presuppose schools operated exclusively by leftists. Yet there are obviously those who do not believe that the role of the schools is social reconstruction. Graff and Cain argue that "in a democratic society the planning of a curriculum sometimes means organizing approaches, ideas, and values that one dislikes." [3]

Finally, there is the matter of the style of much postmodern writing; it is often grindingly turgid, tendentious, repetitious, and lacking in grace and civility. Readers are constantly battered with mind-numbing analyses of power. Admittedly, there are important things to say about the use and abuse of power in a democratic society, but a distinction should be preserved between the legitimate authority intended to secure conditions for teaching and learning and brutal police power that the state wields illegitimately. Aronowitz and Giroux often seem oblivious to this distinction, as they are to the limits of the task Hirsch has set for himself. Hirsch is under no obligation to present an extended explanation of power relations in society. Consequently, the firepower of the critics' heavy ideological artillery is wasted.

I am reminded of voices raised in protest against the abstractions and distortions of ideological thinking. In the introduction to *The Liberal Imagination*, a collection of essays that constituted, among other things, a sympathetic critique of the liberal tradition of intellectual thought and action, Lionel Trilling countered the tendency toward abstraction in ideological thinking with literature's sense of possibility, variousness, complexity, and difficulty.[4] Then there is Richard Hofstadter's observation in *Anti-intellectualism in American Life:* "If there is anything more dangerous to the life of mind than having no independent commitment to ideas, it is having an excess of commitment to some special constricting idea . . . the intellectual function can be overwhelmed by an excess of piety within too contracted a frame of reference."[5] Seeing everything under the aspect of power relations constitutes one such constriction.

In that other famous "two cultures debate," C. P. Snow, like Hirsch, had his share of critics, among whom F. R. Leavis, a British literary intellectual and defender of literary culture, was the most vociferous. In Robert Scholes, a professor of English, Hirsch has his Leavis. Scholes's "Aiming a Canon at the Curriculum" directs dismay and indignation at Hirsch's proposals.[6] The response, however, is yet one more instance of misreading.

Lumping together William Bennett and Hirsch, Scholes sees their positions as an attempt by the federal government to impose a national curriculum on the schools. "Such thinking," he writes, "is of course typical of the political 'right,' which now calls itself 'conservative,' though it might more properly be named 'reactionary.' "[7] Once again intellectual disagreement is cast in political terms. Particularly disconcerted by Bennett's assigning responsibility for the decline in learning to higher education and literary intellectuals, Scholes attacks Bennett for identifying guilty parties, but Scholes himself is not averse to finding villains.

To be sure, Scholes is responding to Hirsch's *American Scholar* article, but, like the critics of *Cultural Literacy* who linked Bloom and Hirsch, he hitches Hirsch to Bennett, with the same misleading consequence. What Bennett took Hirsch to be saying, and what Scholes took both Bennett and Hirsch to be saying, is not what Hirsch was in fact advocating. Indeed, once Bennett realized this, he stopped referring to Hirsch.

In truth, it is Bennett's "To Reclaim a Legacy" that is the principal object of Scholes's criticism.[8] He rejects Bennett's piece on several grounds: for spreading a myth of decline with the intent of paving the way for a powerful leader to set things right; for falsely accusing university presidents and literary intellectuals; and for concealing an ideological perspective that favors powerful hierarchical structures. Scholes further chastizes Bennett for hiding behind a value-free conception of the humanities, which, if true, would drain the humanities of their most distinctive content.

There are several grounds for Scholes's criticism of Hirsch: Hirsch's wish to be taken seriously after having repudiated the research he had conducted for twelve years; the logic of an argument that confuses causes and effects; a failure to distinguish clearly between contextual knowledge acquired in school and that gained outside of school; two conflicting senses of culture (as acculturation and as high culture); the imposition of a common, classical curriculum at the expense of local needs and interests; the notion of cultural literacy as a boon for the producers of tests and crib notes; an inclination to list making; insensitivity to alternative ways of teaching the classics; and the likelihood that teaching will consist of little more than conveying pious clichés about classic texts.

Having fired his cannon, with how many hits shall we credit Scholes? Not too many, for he took wrong aim. Scholes is drawn off-target primarily by his fixation on the teaching of the humanities in higher education and on the problems of identifying and teaching a canon of great books. But as he points out in " 'Cultural Literacy' Does Not Mean 'Canon,' " his response to Scholes, Hirsch was not talking about higher education at all, but about schools. He was not interested in a selection of texts that all school youth should read, but rather in conveying some basic information or facts about some texts (and other things as well) at a rather superficial level. In short, Hirsch did not say, nor does he believe, that a canon of works should be taught to all students.

Accordingly, Hirsch argues, "Although it is true that literacy depends on common background knowledge, it's not true that common background knowledge requires a 'common natural curriculum' or 'canon.' *The common background knowledge required for literacy does not depend upon specific texts,"* and, *"To be culturally literate, one does not need to know any specific literary texts,* though one does need to know a few facts about some of them," all of which is to say that *"the contents of cultural literacy are not text-bound."*[9] So much for the notion of textual authority. Nor is there is any need to fear the regulation of education by a central power.

What Scholes and many of Hirsch's critics miss is the *simplicity* of his ideas and the fact that his principal interest lies in the lower schools, not in college or university education; his concern is primarily with information, not with texts. For all Hirsch cares, this information can be obtained from *Cliff's Notes*. The use of Hirsch's writing for Bennett-bashing then is a misuse. In fact, Hirsch agrees wholeheartedly with Scholes: The selection of texts to be studied should be a local matter, and no text is so trivial as to be beyond humanistic inquiry.

As for the decline of teaching (which Scholes calls a favorite myth of reformers), Hirsch once more refers to the research with which, he claims, all active reading researchers agree, for example, that conducted at the University of Illinois. Richard Anderson, the director of the university's Center for the Study of Reading and, like Scholes, a libertarian, as well as other distinguished researchers, does not see a hidden ideology in Hirsch's concept of cultural literacy; only ideologues have made that inference.[10] The remainder of Hirsch's response consists of detailing the actual decline in literacy, which gives the lie to such decline being a myth. In other words, the data Hirsch cites are impressive and difficult to question. Finally, Hirsch observes the relations of Scholes's own liberal ideology and the class-bound interests of English teachers. True, Hirsch does wonder whether, given its misinterpretation by so many of his colleagues in the field of English, he might have had a problem of communication in his *American Scholar* article. Maybe so. But Hirsch writes simple, direct—that is, good—English, and so there must be other reasons for the distortion of his thesis.

To reply to specific charges contained in Scholes's critique, one might say that Hirsch is credible: He does not confuse cause and effect when he shows the relations between a national literate language and a national literate culture; he is aware that cultural literacy can be acquired informally and tacitly through the cultural environment generally; his concept of culture, with its emphasis on accumulation, is essentially anthropological and thus not to be confused with the high-culture sense of the term; he does not sacrifice local needs and interests (merely subordinates them) in a national literate curriculum; and, a canon of texts being irrelevant, he is sensitive to alternative ways of studying texts. True, Scholes did not have the benefit of Hirsch's discussion of the intensive curriculum in *Cultural Literacy*, but one doubts that it would have made much difference. What seems to disturb Scholes is Hirsch's discussion of core knowledge and a national literate culture, as well as his purported association with a conservative administration.

Having alleged such an association (although, once again, careful readers would find nothing in Hirsch's writings to question his liberal sentiments), critics such as Aronowitz, Giroux, and Scholes have no qualms about deprecating Hirsch by grouping him with extreme, reactionary right-wing thinkers. This is as questionable as classifying all writers who have liberal leanings as radical, left-wing ideologues. Unfortunately, such defamation of character is typical of intellectual life today. This situation suggests that what is needed, as Jacques Barzun wrote in *The House of Intellect*, is not so much a probing of the thoughts of those who have received poor educations, but rather the thoughts of those who have benefited from the very best education—the probing of the anti-intellectualism of the intellectuals—and their intolerance.[11]

In contrast to the critiques of Aronowitz, Giroux, and Scholes, consider George Steiner's review of *Cultural Literacy*.[12] Steiner, a literary intellectual and cultural critic of the first order, first draws attention to the American educational system and its seemingly unstated policy of planned amnesia. Accordingly, "Hirsch is emphatically right," and, the hour being late, his proposal for developing cultural literacy is a necessity. Hirsch's arguable indictments of Rousseau and Dewey are less important to Steiner than the alarming decline in concrete knowledge that Hirsch wants to remedy. Indeed, observes Steiner, "When almost nothing is known, nothing further can be learned." Thus a pressing need exists to recall traditional ideals and practices in order to establish a common readership and a system of minimal shared reference. Rather than dwelling on points made by Hirsch's critics, Steiner draws attention to the spirit that animates Hirsch's book—the spirit expressed in Martin Luther King's "I Have a Dream" speech and in the Jeffersonian ideal "that the greatest possible number of American men and women be educated to the linguistic-contextual level required to read intelligently the news stories and editorial page of a serious, adult newspaper—say, the

Times" (107). Steiner realizes that Hirsch is asking for a canonical performance—intelligent reading and not a commitment to the study of a
canon of great books. Rather than passing over the research that Hirsch
discusses, Steiner accords it proper recognition.

Steiner finds Hirsch's word list fascinating, seeing in it "a peculiarly
graphic image of the American liberal imagination—of the national my-
thologies of common sense—at a certain point in our history" (108)—a
liberal imagination, not, as Aronowitz, Giroux, and Scholes would have
it, a conservative, right-wing imagination. Steiner is not blind to the
political implications of such a list, but he certainly does not regard it
as repressive or reactionary. His critical observations are appropriately
raised after his discussion of the strengths of Hirsch's volume (the way
a review should be written).

Steiner questions Hirsch, who says that the aim of cultural literacy is
to enable people "to thrive in the modern world." Yet this may be difficult, observes Steiner, in a world that has so many unlovely aspects, a remark reflecting his strong conviction that the dark events of the modern
age must not be forgotten. But I think that all Hirsch means by "thrive"
is that people should be able to participate intelligently in discussions
of the events and issues of the day, not that they should be oblivious to
human suffering or enjoy living with pollution and urban blight.

Another of Steiner's criticisms concerns the quality of Hirsch's rhetoric. Steiner, himself an incomparable literary stylist, thinks that a book
on cultural literacy ought to sing with at least some memorable phrases.
But I believe that Hirsch's straightforward, largely descriptive style is
a conscious choice. It is a reaction, on the one hand, to the excessively florid prose of much writing in the humanities, and, on the other,
to the density of prose in postmodern theorizing. (Some literary one-
upmanship on the part of Steiner is undoubtedly also at work.) Overall, Steiner pays Hirsch a high compliment for intelligently addressing
a serious problem that has preoccupied Steiner himself, the problem of
cultural amnesia.

Other critical responses convey something of the temper and mood that
a book such as Hirsch's can engender. To those who object that literate
persons are more than the sum of the allusions they command and are
instead simply people who want to read another book, Hirsch would reply that, without a system of shared allusions, no one is likely to read

very well. Revisionists who say that conservative restoration has betrayed the interpretation of American education that grew out of the countercultural sixties overstate the case; some kind of reaction was inevitable as revisionists kept raising the stakes. Unable to accommodate themselves to anything less than revolutionary change, revisionists further beg credibility by turning patronizing and vindictive whenever their ideas meet resistance—an attitude that itself reveals an underlying authoritarianism and elitism. But what is truly elitist, writes Christopher Clausen, is the revisionists' assumption that "a stew of popular culture, social indoctrination, and a selection of recent American writing provides sufficient intellectual nourishment for students who lack the advantages of an upper-middle-class childhood." [13]

The presumption of superiority of such critics is also partly to blame for the numerous errors and misrepresentations in their interpretations of the writings with which they disagree. Convinced of the correctness of their revolutionary thinking, they lack the appreciation of difficulty and complexity evident in all good criticism. What radical criticism fails to acknowledge is that without some conserving function there would be no way to transmit the information, skills, and values that are imperative for living in the modern world. Among those things and values worth preserving, writes Roger Shattuck, are a profound sense of continuity in human life and the visions of greatness embodied in masterworks. In defense of the study of the classics, Shattuck writes that "a classic will make its historical moment vivid and important; it will also have other features that make it remain contemporary. In other words, it is at the same time a period piece and forever young." What is more, a masterwork is at once simple and clear as well as complex and mysterious and may thus be reassuring as well as intimidating, as is the case with Tolstoy's *The Death of Ivan Ilyich*. Finally, a classic will "create the sense of continuing concrete, individual situations and characters, which at the same time reach toward the domain of the general, the universal. In her best poems, Emily Dickinson's literary persona becomes a very concrete universal." [14]

In Hirsch's theory of education, the study of classics would occur during the intensive curriculum, the secondary years of schooling, that portion of a two-part curriculum that most of Hirsch's readers either fail to notice or fail to accord proper attention. Hirsch allows for considerable freedom of choice about what to study in the intensive curriculum—a freedom that got him into trouble with other critics, who would prefer that he be as specific about the intensive as about the extensive curriculum.

Although the foregoing has defended Hirsch against critics who have either misunderstood him or taken his book as an opportunity to superimpose their own ideas on his, it may still be true that Hirsch bears some responsibility for being misunderstood. His discussion of the two spheres that exist with respect to cultural literacy—one of the culturally literate and the other of the functionally and culturally illiterate—displays some of the tendencies exemplified by C. P. Snow in his lecture "The Two Cultures and the Scientific Revolution," which instigated more than a decade of debate. Because of these similarities, Hirsch could have subtitled his book "The Two Cultures and the Cognitive Revolution in Language." Snow's message, simple and practical though it was, was largely misunderstood, and the disputes that ensued revealed several features of what Bertrand de Jouvenal calls the "ecology of ideas." [15]

De Jouvenal ponders the possibility of taking a census of ideas that could be classified in different ways. Minds would be inspected with a view to ascertaining how many of them contained a particular idea or some semblance of it—some of the names and concepts on Hirsch's word list, for example. The result would not only be some indication of populations that did or did not have such contents in their minds, but also which ideas were gaining or losing ground. In Hirsch's view, the general background information that Americans need for understanding and communicating is noticeably losing ground, while localized, particularized, parochial information is gaining. Such a census, says de Jouvenal, would also enable us to learn something about the competition among ideas, the ways, for example, that new ideas are received with various degrees of acceptance and hostility into different environments, as was the case with Snow's and Hirsch's ideas. De Jouvenal thinks that if it were actually possible to survey the ecosystem of ideas, then we might be in a better position to identify those ideas that might be embraced in the future and conjecture about their fate. Ideas, being important determinants of action, invite inquiry into their origins, careers, and possible futures.

Different kinds of ideas are also accorded different kinds of reception. Social, moral, and cultural ideas are usually more susceptible to controversy than scientific ideas, the criteria for deciding the merit of the latter being more widely accepted. Generally, an extended period of testing and confirmation is necessary for scientific ideas to become part of scientific knowledge. But this is not always the case with social ideas; in a very short time they may come to exert a powerful influence within society, as has, for instance, the notion of multiculturalism.

As one example of the reception of an idea, de Jouvenal reviewed the reaction to *The Origin of Species.* Darwin's propositions were either rejected or accepted, depending on how they interacted with existing ideas. More precisely, there were selective responses by different groups who found that Darwin's ideas either supported their values and aspirations or constituted a threat. The acceptance that science achieved by midcentury certainly prepared the soil for Snow's recommendations for developing greater scientific rationality. Some writers claimed that there was only one culture, the scientific, and that scientific rationality was society's operative religion. Yet Snow's educational recommendations and his analysis of the two cultures encountered great resistance from the community of literary intellectuals (at least they constituted themselves into a community in their criticism of Snow). This is understandable; just as Hirsch holds Rousseau, Dewey, and progressive educationists responsible for the decline of cultural literacy, so Snow held literary intellectuals culpable for their purported romantic and reactionary attitudes toward science, technology, and the future.

Both Snow and Hirsch were probably wrong to characterize their villains in such bold strokes. Yet what concerns and interests me about the two-cultures debate is also, at least in part, what interests me about the cultural literacy debate: How were Hirsch's ideas received, discussed, disputed, applied, and extended? How did the ideas move through different populations? With what other ideas did they come into conflict? What, to use de Jouvenal's terminology, were Hirsch's general ideas and their particular propositions? Charting the reception and fate of Snow's ideas was rather simple, as its course was punctuated by fairly specific events: the initial impact of his lecture, including F. R. Leavis's reaction, Snow's second look at his analysis, and his third look printed in a later collection of his essays. More recently, the debate was recalled by Roger Scruton in a discussion of aesthetics and culture that also relates to the cultural literacy debate.[16]

So far as the reception of *Cultural Literacy* is concerned, there was the impact of the book on the popular media, Hirsch's academic colleagues, the general population, and interested agencies and foundations. (As I suggested earlier, Leavis's attack on Snow found its counterpart in

Scholes's critique of Hirsch.) Then there was the flurry of articles that Hirsch wrote to further explain what he had and had not said. In the meantime, he founded the Foundation for Cultural Literacy (a name later changed to Core Knowledge) for the purpose of implementing his ideas. He also published a dictionary of cultural literacy and a number of subsequent materials (including tests and graded dictionaries that are beginning to appear) and a newsletter that reports on efforts to raise the level of cultural literacy—all this since 1987, when *Cultural Literacy* appeared. Unlike the participants in the two-cultures debate who kept things mainly on the verbal plane, Hirsch has taken the challenge to raise cultural literacy into the schools and the mass media.[17]

Snow's general ideas consisted of the moral obligation of rich countries to help poor ones and the practical need to reform education in order to achieve a common culture that included scientific literacy. Hirsch's general ideas in *Cultural Literacy* concerned (1) the moral obligation to break the cycles of illiteracy, poverty, and social injustice that afflict deprived children and to extend to all members of society the opportunity to participate in the political process (in short, the Jeffersonian ideal); and (2) the need to provide the young with a common literate culture that would enable them to function more effectively in society. Yet, like Snow, whose appeal was limited by his uncomplimentary remarks about the moral qualities of literary humanists, Hirsch's proposals were handicapped by the fact that he named pedagogical villains. This strategy obviously did not sit well with many educationists and was considered arguable even by some of Hirsch's academic colleagues. Although the temptation is understandable, it seems ill-advised to criticize figures held in high regard by those who must ultimately help implement reforms. Certainly, Hirsch did not make himself popular with those educators who had expressed concerns similar to his but who remained anonymous in his writings. Nonetheless, just as Snow's discussion stimulated a renewed interest in the epistemology of the sciences and the humanities—the question of the kinds of knowledge that these two realms of human enterprise generate—so Hirsch stimulated a debate on the common elements of a national literate culture. His concern, however, was not essentially epistemological; it was simply with the minimal general information that literate persons possess.

Yet another similarity obtains between the two cultures and the cultural literacy debates. As pointed out, Snow's characterization of the moral obligation of wealthy nations to provide aid to poor countries as the most pressing concern was lost in the controversy over the nature of the scientific and the literary cultures. Similarly, Hirsch's urging to break the cycle of illiteracy in society was drowned in the uproar about his list and the rote, replicative learning it seemed to require. Later, Snow acknowledged that perhaps his strategy was partly to blame; there was, for example, a certain lack of tact in his thesis. Hirsch has likewise had second thoughts and wondered whether the term *cultural literacy* was the most felicitous for his purposes. I also think that Hirsch was mistaken in not bringing up the two-part curriculum—extensive and intensive—earlier in his argument. The discussion of the intensive curriculum, for example, does not come until page 128 of his 145-page text. Although some readers obviously read that far, Hirsch apparently conveyed the impression that the extensive curriculum was the whole of schooling, when in fact it constitutes only part of the early years. He considered his definition of the extensive curriculum his major contribution, but, unfortunately, it was equated with the whole of schooling. Consequently, Hirsch has had to clarify over and over what he meant, in particular that he was not recommending a canon of works.

That Hirsch's concern to meliorate the conditions of deprived children was either ignored or not taken seriously is perhaps also attributable to the fact that he did not dramatize the moral aspects of his argument sufficiently. Then, like some of Snow's statements that struck his readers as dubious (for example, that the mindset of literary intellectuals actually rules the Western world), Hirsch's emphatic characterization of much of the contents of cultural literacy as superficial and vague undoubtedly invited ridicule. I rather imagine that he regrets having said that only a few hundred pages separate the culturally illiterate from the culturally literate. Why then all the fuss? Projected into an educational environment in which the so-called higher-level thought processes—creativeness, critical thinking, problem solving, and so forth—are all the rage, Hirsch's ideas were bound to sound pedestrian. Yet because he was intentionally challenging thought-clichés about teaching and learning, Hirsch deliberately kept his discussion low-keyed and centered it on the fundamentals upon which the higher cognitive activities depend. When his work is read carefully, most of what critics thought was missing is actually there.

The cultural literacy debate exhibits all of the characteristics associated with the acceptance, rejection, and extension of ideas. Hirsch's moral and practical ideas were received into a partly friendly, partly hostile environment, where they made—and are making—their way through the population, compounding with some ideas and engaging others in debate. As in the case of Snow, discussion of the practical consequences of Hirsch's ideas upstaged discussions of his moral concerns.

Today, the controversy over cultural literacy has subsided, and practical work is quietly underway, including Hirsch's efforts to implement his ideas. The larger debate, which is carried on in a highly politicized atmosphere, concerns literacy itself and the social functions of literacy.

The Arts and
Contextual Knowledge

Hɪʀsᴄʜ's *Cultural Literacy* is about reading and writing, especially about the background knowledge people need to read a newspaper intelligently and communicate with others effectively. Because newspapers contain discussions of the arts, background knowledge about art is needed to make sense of what is reported. Yet this is difficult to do if readers lack a common language of understanding. Indeed, it is difficult to think of someone as culturally literate who does not command some general knowledge of artists, artworks, and the art world. Not surprisingly then, several items about art appear on Hirsch's word list and in a section on the arts in his *Dictionary of Cultural Literacy* and subsequent publications.[1]

Still, as it applies to the arts, the concept of cultural literacy calls for more specific definition and searching reflection. Toward that end, I invited, as part of the study described in the Introduction, contributors from aesthetics (the philosophy of art), literature, the visual arts, music, theater, and educational theory (the philosophy of education) to speculate about the import of Hirsch's ideas for arts education. This was one more way of moving his ideas through different populations, where they could be further scrutinized, applied, modified, and extended. Hirsch provided the opening essay for the special issue of the *Journal of Aesthetic Education* (Spring 1990) in which the contributions first appeared, and the issue was subsequently published in book form.[2]

Hirsch begins "Reflections about Cultural Literacy and Arts Education" by asking whether the concept of cultural literacy, a practical, utilitarian notion, has anything to contribute to the teaching of art.[3] The question arises in light of the tendency of theorists to justify arts education programs by claiming that they promote the appreciation of the intrinsic and nonutilitarian values of art. But Hirsch suggests that so long as arts educators cling to an argument from intrinsic value, arts education may be perceived as achieving little more than enlivening cocktail party chatter. Indeed, Hirsch thinks that arts educators needlessly and harmfully underplay the utility of their efforts. "Yet surely it is both a spiritual and utilitarian value to bind members of a society together through common experiences in all domains of life, including the domains of art—enough common experiences to enable the broadest possible communication and cooperation among its members." There need not be conflict, in other words, between the goals of the aesthetic educator and those of the social pragmatist: "Art education, which elevates the soul of the individual, also contributes to social solidarity." Although solidarity does not necessarily require uniform attitudes toward the arts, the virtues of individuality and pluralism can be fully realized only within a context of community and social cohesion.

Hirsch, as others have done, is helpful in drawing attention to the ambiguity inherent in the notion of intrinsic value. Instead of positing something called intrinsic value, which implies that some things can be valued for their own sake, he believes that we should locate the arts along a continuum of instrumental values. If, as is commonly believed, art has the capacity to shape human emotion and thought, then it certainly has instrumental efficacy.

Given Hirsch's disposition regarding the urgency of practical educational reform, it is not surprising that he eschews florid rhetoric and the usual platitudes that abound in talk about art. His advice to arts educators is to be more precise in stipulating the basic information that all young people should have. Learning in the arts should go beyond the development of an aesthetic sense and include the study of specific artists and artworks. Consistent with his definition of cultural literacy as the core knowledge of mainstream culture, however, Hirsch must conclude that the information to be conveyed should not only be about artistically excellent works—although there are a few that he thinks everyone should know—but also about those that have become well known simply by historical accident. Thus both Grant Wood's *American Gothic* and Botticelli's *The Birth of Venus*, Currier and Ives and John Constable,

Gilbert and Sullivan and Giacomo Puccini, and so forth, are found in Hirsch's lexicon.

Yet Hirsch acknowledges that arts education has an additional obligation to help raise culture above its current level. In the past, the inspiration for improving the quality of art and taste has traditionally come from the great critics—the Vasaris, the Berensons, the Roger Frys, and their counterparts in the other arts—those who have had the power to persuade others about what is worth experiencing. In our day, such critics have been joined by numerous prophets of cultural change, whom Hirsch challenges to make it their project "to be just as specific about the shared curriculum as are the proponents of cultural literacy" (6). Yet Hirsch sees little evidence of anyone taking on this task, an assessment that is perhaps not quite accurate.

Several other essays from *Cultural Literacy and Arts Education* provide illuminating commentaries on, and amplifications of, Hirsch's ideas, particularly with respect to the intensive curriculum, where the concept of cultural literacy becomes more prescriptive. The contributors were asked to reflect on the extent to which they thought contextual knowledge can help reveal the character of artwork, a question suggested by Peter Winch's essay "Text and Context" in *Trying to Make Sense*.[4] Some contributors discussed the question more or less explicitly, whereas others addressed different aspects of Hirsch's thesis.

Perhaps it is helpful to think of cultural literacy in two senses: the thin sense (the extensive curriculum) and the thick sense (the intensive curriculum). Relying on a student's knowledge of the thin sense of cultural literacy, the intensive curriculum deals more explicitly with the problem of raising the level of the current culture. It does not attempt to do so directly, for example through the political indoctrination of young people with radical cultural ideas, but indirectly by cultivating a better understanding of art and an appreciation of its greatest works. This indirect approach assumes that persons who have acquired a disposition to prize excellence in art will be more likely to become impatient with inferior art and a shabby habitat.

In "Contexts of Dance," Francis Sparshott systematically sets out the minimal contextual knowledge required for understanding dance as an art.[5] Indeed, his discussion is a model for thinking about the contexts needed to understand other art forms.

A Canadian, Sparshott first fires a volley of "Sparshotts" (as his observations are sometimes called) across the border to strike at problems with Hirsch's notion of mainstream culture (which Sparshott calls "imperial" culture). Can it really be the case, he asks, that literate Americans need know so little about Canada and practically nothing about dance? That is precisely what the sparsity of references to dance in Hirsch's list implies. Sparshott begins his discussion by drawing attention to the numerous programs about dance shown on television, from which one can learn a lot.

> First, there is the basic readiness to attend to the ways in which movements are put together so as to be danceable and a sensitivity to what is possible and what is not as well as to what is effective and what is not. Second, there is the double awareness that dance is strenuous and demands great skill and trained strength, but also that that is not what a dance is actually about. Third, most important, there is the awareness that people who make dances are very serious about dancing and dancemaking, that they give thought to what they are doing, they are not just waving their arms and legs. Fourth, also important, the fact that the series is shown on network television (even if "only" on an educational or public network) testifies that we ourselves can also be expected to take dance seriously as an activity in the public realm. (77–78)

All of this is appropriate contextual knowledge. But what, more specifically and yet still generally, does one have to know about dance? Clearly, one needs a mental sorting office stocked with a large number of facts, names, and classificatory schemata that can place dance in relation to other human activities. And one should also have frameworks of expectations with regard to dance itself in order to get what is relevant out of it.

Further helpful, Sparshott distinguishes three kinds of dances that one can experience in America: social dances, ethnic dances, and art dances. Social dances are part of the mating game and an endorsement of togetherness, whereas ethnic dances are part of a way of life in which they play either a structural or an ideological role. Art dances are part of the art world and its characteristic concerns. These types of dances often overlap, and people may take them up for different reasons. One should know the conventions that govern social dance, and what it means and says about people when they perform it in certain ways (disco dancing is Sparshott's example). One should also know that there is such a thing as ethnic dancing, which can usually be understood outside the context of the art world. When ethnic dances enter into the venues of the art world, the question becomes whether they remain purely ethnic dances, for they no longer perform some of their basic functions, for example, those bound up with the pride and identity of a specific subculture. Given the contemporary awareness of global-villagism, Sparshott thinks that some general knowledge about ethnic dances should be part of a person's cultural literacy. (He observes that McLuhan's "global village" makes Hirsch's word list, but "multiculturalism" does not.)

Sparshott's principal concern, however, is with dance as art and not as a form of recreation or an affirmation of personal or cultural identity. What are the contextual requirements for understanding dance this way? Just what one might expect; the most important is the ability to take an art stance (or to assume an aesthetic attitude) toward something. It is instructive, moreover, to see dance-as-art against the backdrop of the generic sense of dance as "nonfunctional movement of the human body, considered in two ways: as something a person can do and as something a person can watch." That is, "people are dancing when they are moving to no practical purpose" (79–80).

Taking an art stance toward dance presupposes a system of expectations that derives from both cultural history and current practices. In particular, because there are different kinds of art dances—ballet, modern, contemporary, postmodern, and experimental—an art stance further implies knowing the conventions and restraints of each type.

> The essential context of dance-as-art, then, is that of the art world, and immediately the concept of a work of art. The dominant idea is that a dance of the sort in question is to be *looked at* as an object for appreciation—and, more specifically, to be looked at in the way one looks at and listens to a dramatic performance or listens to a piece of music being played. That is different from the sympathetic or satiric interest with which one watches one's fellow dancers while one takes a breather in a social dance; from the sort of lateral appreciation of oneself and one's fellows in a dance in which all are joined; from the self-immersion in a ceremony in which one participates and in which dance is a component. It is very complicated, involving measures of absorption and of critical distancing, of attention and self-loss, in ways that are familiar

and controversial at the same time—it is being subject to just those controversies that is most characteristic of our transactions with works of art as such. (82)

Reading Sparshott thus reminds one of Hirsch's observation that schemata (classificatory systems) are related to schemata that are related to still more schemata. Of what contextual considerations need one be aware to assume the art stance?

To take an art stance toward dance presupposes the possession of a threefold schema that, as Sparshott argues, takes into consideration the formal or material, mimetic or referential, and expressive aspects of artworks. In addition, one can hold

> that it is essential to the appreciation of art that one bring to it some sense of art making as serious work, as opposed to self-expression or amusement or self-advertisement. The seriousness of art as an activity is certainly an essential part of our understanding of what art is. Other demands are made. One needs to be aware at some level and in some fashion of the relation of artworks to the social organizations in which they are produced and enjoyed: not that one must have any particular view on this matter, but that one must be aware that it is a matter on which views may importantly be held. And one must be aware, in some fashion and at some level, of the expectations that govern the relation of artworks to the traditions of production: the demand for originality, the prevalence of genres and influences. This whole mass of relationships is largely constitutive of what art as art is and holds equally of all arts. One can indeed deny that some of these considerations are truly relevant or important; but one cannot reasonably deny that they are all part of what is deemed central to art by some of those who speak with most authority. (83–84)

What Americans should know about dance in America is its historical development from classical ballet to modern dance and the relations in which modern dance stands to it and to contemporary, postmodern, and experimental dance. (Sparshott avoids the use of the term *avant-garde*.) In other words, the ability to assume an art stance involves knowing not only what traditionally has constituted such a stance but also those instances in which it is being creatively extended or rejuvenated, perhaps even repudiated. Sparshott helps readers locate themselves along a continuum of how art audiences tend to behave and what they prize and think of themselves:

1. Ballet. Look for technique. Pride self on connoisseurship. Associate with aristocracy or reasonable facsimile.
2. Modern. Look for expression of inner self. Pride self on dedication to art. Associate with professional bourgeoisie.
3. Contemporary. Look for artistry concealing itself. Pride self on being with it. Associate with the art world.
4. Postmodern. Look for joky allusions. Pride self on not priding self. Associate with the up-and-coming.
5. Experimental. Look for anything, including nothing. Pride self on being ahead of the rush. Associate with the studio world. (85)

At this point I recall an educational conference in Great Britain at which dancers from the Festival Ballet Theater demonstrated some typical patterns of the ballet. During a question-and-answer session I had a friend ask the dancers what they thought it was that the uninformed ballet-goer is likely to miss. The dancers replied that there was very little to know; one needed only to enjoy the performance. ("A daft question deserves a daft answer," my friend whispered to me.) Yet surely there is a point to ballet. And Sparshott states what it is:

> There is little point in seeing a ballet, for instance, unless one grasps two things: the extreme nature of the demands placed upon the body, both in terms of the initial preparation and deformation and in terms of the continually rigorous regime; and the prevailing belief that the body is thus *ennobled* by grace and strength. The reason why this double ideology is essential is that it is unlikely to be evident, since the effect of the training is to make itself invisible, and to look at what is going on as a merely pretty flouncing around can result only in facile wonder or boredom. The preparedness for a rigorous intensity and a willingness to accept that as spiritually justified are what one has to bring with one. . . . [T]hat is part of the presumption of intense seriousness that is required by the idea of art as such; but it is something more, a devotion to the refinement and exaltation of human corporeality. (85–86)

Is the paradigm of a culturally literate lover of dance one who prefers one type of dance over another, say, classical ballet in preference to modern dance, postmodern over modern dance, or experimental over postmodern dance? Cultural literacy, says Sparshott, does not rule out partisanship, but it does require that one at least be aware of alternatives and able to assume a relevant stance toward them. Furthermore, it contributes to understanding rather than harms it to have some sociological information about the dynamics of dance audiences, their variegated composition, and some reasons why things are as they are: Someone is making decisions and pulling strings behind the performances. Although such knowledge may not always be directly relevant to the experience of dance, it seems to be something that a culturally literate person would know.

But with so much to know, even in a general way, about the contexts of dance, what is the special responsibility of the schools? Their role would be the same as it is toward art in general—to provide orientation and perspective by developing relevant interpretive and appreciative capacities. This can be done, first, by ensuring a minimum system of common, shared associations regarding dance in the thin sense of cultural literacy (which may also be called the surface sense of cultural literacy) and, second, by paying attention to the thick sense implied by Sparshott's account of the contexts of dance (the deeper sense of cultural literacy). Hirsch's and Sparshott's accounts of cultural literacy both exist in a relation of shallow relief to deep relief; they exist at different levels of depth but are joined inextricably.

Sparshott takes note of Hirsch's assertion that the concept of cultural literacy, although largely traditional and stable, nonetheless has the potential for change. He also understands Hirsch to be saying that the rise of enclavism in society threatens the perpetuation of the mainstream culture and the basic, common perspective it provides. But given the prominence of dance in American culture and the fact that the history of modern dance is largely American, Sparshott wonders why Hirsch's lexicon contains so few references to dance. I do not know how Hirsch would respond. Perhaps he would acknowledge such lacunae in his lexicon, or perhaps he would simply say, "That's the way it is with culturally literate Americans." Whatever his reaction, it is obvious that he would locate the obligation to foster most relevant contextual knowledge about dance within the intensive curriculum. Sparshott, who makes it clear that a lot of specific knowledge about dancers, dance practice, and dance performances must be conveyed to secure understanding of what is going on in dance-as-art, probably would agree with Hirsch that a content-neutral pedagogy is inadequate to the job.

The contextual knowledge that Sparshott thinks is necessary for understanding dance-as-art is summarized by the following propositions: (1) dance is worth knowing about, in fact, culturally literate persons should know more about it than Hirsch's lexicon indicates; (2) even though dance goes against the genre of American mainstream culture, dance as practiced in America says something important about America and Americans; (3) there is a great deal of overlap between dance in mainstream America and in its subcultures, and as far as dance is concerned the localism of subcultures is perhaps not quite the problem Hirsch takes it to be; (4) one should understand the nature and function of dance-as-art against the backdrop of the generic concept of dance; (5) one should be able to place dance among the various activities of the mainstream culture, which presupposes a mental sorting capacity to assign certain kinds of activity to interpret situations appropriately; (6) one can learn a lot about dance by watching television, the vehicle that perhaps more than any other makes dance accessible; (7) one can distinguish art dance from social and ethnic dance, even though they have similarities and the perspective of one may be superimposed on another; (8) in placing dance one needs to call on an indefinitely large set of facts, names, and classificatory schemata, including schemata of expectations that derive from the current presuppositions of the art world and an understanding of what it is to regard something from an art stance; (9) the schema useful for responding to dance-as-art is also relevant to assuming an art stance toward any object (one that draws attention to the formal, referential, and expressive aspects of artworks); (10) the emergence of modern dance must be understood against the tradition of classical ballet, and modern dance in relation to contemporary, postmodern, and experimental dance; (11) accordingly, although one may admire one particular kind of dance, a culturally literate person should also know how to accommodate and understand alternative dances; (12) some sociological information is also helpful, for example, about how the decision making dynamics of the art world affect which works get staged and who goes to watch them; and (13) simple, relatively uninformed enjoyment of dance is not likely to reward the effort or expenditure invested in attending dance performances nearly as well as does a response guided and energized by relevant and background information.

Once more, Hirsch conceives schemata as being stored in the mind's short-term and long-term memory for later recall and use. They consist of clusters of ideas related by superordination and subsumption, as is the case with schemata relating to mainstream culture and its subcultures. As for dance, there are schemata about types of dance, including the notion of generic dancing, and others about dance-as-art, types of art dance, the history and sociology of dance, and so forth.

The special merit of Sparshott's contribution to *Cultural Literacy and Arts Education* lies in how it provides a model for thinking about the contexts of any art. For example, I now see better than I did before reading Sparshott what is involved in building a sense of art in the young.[6] Sparshott's essay also complements nicely and goes beyond an informative article by Henry Aiken, who also discusses the preconditions for understanding and appreciating works of art appropriately, the preconditions, for example, for experiencing Giorgione's *The Tempest*.[7]

Sparshott provides a systematic account of the contextual knowledge needed by literate Americans in order to understand and appreciate dance and share their experiences of it. In "Musical Literacy," Jerrold Levinson, a philosopher of art who has a technical knowledge of music, sets himself a similar task but approaches it with different twists and accents.[8] Recognizing the relevance of schema theory to musical literacy, Levinson distinguishes musical literacy in its narrow sense, that is, Hirsch's sense, and in a broader sense he calls "comprehending listening." Just as Hirsch wants persons to be able to understand verbal utterances, Levinson explores what is involved in understanding musical utterances. "Understanding a piece of music," he writes, "is fundamentally hearing it in an appropriate way, in virtue of the experiences one has had and the resulting reorganization of one's mental space, whereas understanding a written text remains grasping an articulate meaning, even if this involves effecting an integration (as Hirsch insists) between the statements of the text and a larger body of knowledge discursively possessed" (24).

Levinson provides an example of musical literacy in a sketch of what a comprehending listener (CL) does, hears, or experiences in listening for the first time to the first movement of Bruckner's Fourth Symphony (E-flat):

> (1) A CL hears the music as *tonal*, i.e., as constructed on the basis of a familiar set of eight-note scales, major and minor, and as having certain implied standards of consonance and dissonance—or stability and instability—both melodically and harmonically. (2) A

CL hears the music as *symphonic*, i.e., as a large-scale utterance, with regard to both span of time and number of voices or parts involved. (3) A CL hears the music as *Romantic* (or nineteenth-century) in style, i.e., having certain distinctive features and ways of developing which that term denotes. (4) A CL hears the music as roughly in *sonata form*. (5) A CL hears the music as specifically *Brucknerian* in character. (6) A CL has an experience of the connectedness of the music—of its individual *motion or flow or progression*—rather than merely one of discrete, momentary sounds in succession. (7) A CL has a series of appropriate reactions and registerings on the order of *tension and release*, or *expectation and fulfillment*, or *implication and realization* during the course of the music. (8) A CL hears the music's progression with some awareness of the *performance means* (or performing acts) involved in generating the sounds being heard. (9) A CL apprehends in large measure the *gestural and emotional* content of the music. (10) A CL has a sense of the *wider resonances*—in this case, mythic, religious, and nature-loving ones—attaching to the movement, rightly construed. (19–20)

Quite a lot to know, one might say, for general musical literacy, but Levinson is talking about musical literacy in its thick, or deep, sense and about instruction that conveys more than superficial understanding and would therefore typically be found in Hirsch's intensive curriculum. Levinson is equally informative when he details what listeners would miss or misconstrue in the Bruckner movement if they did not hear the music as tonal, symphonic, romantic, in sonata form, and so forth. The point is that listening to music appropriately depends heavily on contextual knowledge. For music to be heard or experienced properly, it must "be related to—brought in some fashion into juxtaposition with—patterns, norms, phenomena, facts, lying outside the specific music itself" (22). Referring to the passage quoted above, Levinson writes:

Thus, to hear the movement as tonal (1) is to hear it in relation, however implicitly, to an underlying scale and range of chords; and hearing the specific moment-to-moment flow and connectedness (6) in a movement such as this can hardly be separated from hearing it tonally. To hear the movement as symphonic (2) is to compare it with a template of features applicable to other symphonies and drawn from them; to hear the movement as "sonataing" (4) is to bring to bear on the music as it unfolds a general schema of sonata form, with which the music can be seen to comply more or less, though in its own individual, and sometimes temporarily deceptive, way. To hear it as Romantic (3) or Brucknerian (5) in character is obviously to connect it with other works of music by the composer, his contemporaries, and his predecessors. To hear the music not as disembodied tones but as the upshot of human actions applied to physical devices (8) means, among other things, gauging musical events with respect to the dynamic ranges of the various instruments (e.g., brass vs. woodwinds vs. strings), which ranges are not transparently displayed in the piece at hand. To have the right series of expectations, the right awareness of implications and realizations, the right sense of the rise and fall of tensions in the course of the movement (7), can come about only if one is perceiving the music against the backdrop of a host of norms associated with the style, genre, and period categories, and the individual compositional corpus, to which the movement belongs.

This leaves only (9) and (10), a CL's appreciation of the "extra-musical" content, if we may call it that, of Bruckner's musical essay. Can there be any doubt that this cannot fully emerge in the absence of connections made by the listener between sequences of sound and broad spheres of human life lying wholly outside the notes themselves? (22)

Once again,

> To be musically literate thus requires internally classifying pieces as they are being heard in certain apt ways. And this, inescapably, means relating the given piece to a background repertoire of other pieces that have been heard and stored—whether as such or in condensed and abstracted form as archetypes, paradigms, and patterns of probabilities. It is this extensive background of what has been heard earlier, on other occasions, in addition to what has been internalized concerning relevant contexts external to music, which confronts each piece of music new to a literate listener, enabling it to be received in a manner that counts—though sometimes only after a second and third hearing—as understanding. Comprehending listening is a process of constant, largely unconscious correlation, and a listener without a "past" will be incapable of having it go on in him in the right way. (27)

I have quoted Levinson extensively because, like Sparshott, he sets out matters clearly, systematically, and informatively in ways that paraphrase cannot do justice. But Levinson goes beyond Sparshott to discuss more specifically pedagogical questions, for example, how to teach the differences between verbal utterances and musical utterances and the comprehension of each. The basic task is to understand how factual knowledge about music functions in comprehending listening and how much of it should be taught explicitly and systematically to cultivate appropriate listening habits.

Another way to put the matter is to ask what role propositional knowledge plays in developing musical literacy in prospective listeners and how such knowledge should be acquired. Here Levinson seems somewhat ambivalent, holding that articulate, propositional knowledge has a role to play and that musical listening habits should be acquired intuitively or tacitly through hearing music repeatedly. Factual knowledge— names of composers, styles, musical forms, works themselves—may trigger relevant schemata, which are forged and reshaped mainly through intensive listening. What does one need to know, Levinson asks, in order to be a comprehending listener in a tradition, for example the tradition of Western classical music? His conclusions have an important bearing on the way music is taught.

Levinson's first point is that although the knowledge about the Bruckner movement—about its tonality, romantic style, musical form, and place in Bruckner's work—is necessary for comprehending listening, it does not have to be known in propositional form or learned through explicit, verbally mediated instruction. Such knowledge need not be available in discursive dress. "The relevant background knowledge of a CL may be largely *tacit*, not explicit," argues Levinson, "and he may often come to a lot of it in a largely *intuitive*, experiential, non-verbally-mediated way" (24). That matters are different with reading literacy is the import of the earlier citation containing Levinson's definition of musical understanding.

> A musically literate individual in the sense under consideration— that is, listening literacy—need never have digested a formal definition of concerto or fugue, need never have grasped the least fundamental of harmonic theory, need not know how many octaves and fractions thereof each orchestral instrument spans, need not be able to tick off the characteristics of Baroque style. He need

only have an implicit grasp of these things—in his bones and ears, so to speak. His literacy ultimately resides in a set of experientially induced, context-sensitive dispositions to respond appropriately to musical events in specific settings, and not in items of recoverable information in a mental dictionary of musical matters. Being musically literate is being sensitive to differences, departures, and digressions, relative to internalized norms of style, genre, and form. It is responding to secondary features of musical structure—timbre, tempo, dynamics, phrasing—in a way framed by awareness of the physicality of the instruments which make that structure sound. It may even involve, in some cases, appreciation of the individual answer to an old quandary carried by a given piece of music, a solution to an artistic problem implicit in its sequence of predecessors. But in every instance, comprehension is essentially *appropriate construal*, and not—or not necessarily—*intellectual realization*, and must thus rest fundamentally on a history of aural absorption as opposed to conscious cogitation. (24–25)

The rest of Levinson's explanation of appropriate construal (in contrast to intellectual realization), although not difficult to understand, again resists simple paraphrase and summarization, but I shall try. I take Levinson to emphasize that one cannot learn to listen to music merely by reading about it, that even the most complete understanding of the words used to explain, say, sonata form, is no aid to an appreciation of what a composer has done with this form in a given instance. To be sure, guided listening is the key to musical comprehension and involves recourse to relevant indicators and verbal descriptions but only to the extent that they help reveal the audible character of a sonata composition. Conceivably, one could pass an examination on verbal explanations of the sonata form without ever having heard a sonata.

What goes for learning to perceive the sonata form goes as well for other musical forms and the technical aspects of music. The minimally required amount of specific, technical knowledge is quite negligible in comparison with the bulk of information that is acquired tacitly and known implicitly. One learns to hear classical music by becoming absorbed in it under proper guidance. In this way the standard or normal characteristics of composers and works become internalized, knowledge that is tacitly brought to bear in listening to an individual work. Once a sufficient degree of musical literacy has been attained, even brief cues—

a few bars of music, a date, a composer's name, or the name of a musical form—will be enough to trigger relevant schemata, expectations, and associations. All of this is possible because, unlike reading literacy, musical literacy is "primarily tacit, nondiscursive, not propositionally expressible and exhibitable" (27).

Levinson believes that "it is the laying down of habits of response and construal, and not the laying in of descriptive information, that remains the real work of converting a musically illiterate ear into a musically literate one" (27). The way to come by the contextual knowledge (formal, stylistic, historical, expressive, and instructional) that will serve one well in future listening is through intensive listening. Does this mean that Levinson would prefer, as opposed to Hirsch, a content-neutral skills approach—inculcation of merely the habits and attitudes of comprehending listening—to the development of cultural literacy? At first blush it might seem so, but Levinson is specific concerning the contextual information required for comprehending listening, and this makes him a genuine contextualist. Comprehending listening presupposes a background repertoire of pieces whose schemata have been internalized and stored through careful listening. What I think Levinson wants to caution against is overintellectualization and overreliance on specification and verbalization in music education, practices that obscure rather than render audible the values of music. Perhaps the consequence of Levinson's suggestions would be that extensive information (acquired during the early years), along with some relevant musical activities, help the young not only to enter mainstream culture but also to develop the disposition for comprehending listening that is the goal of the intensive curriculum (habits and ideas acquired during the secondary years).

Hirsch believes that theorists of the intensive curriculum, like those of the extensive curriculum, have an obligation to be as explicit as possible. Levinson agrees that one must know about relevant contexts of music in order to construe music appropriately. His special concern is how the young acquire this contextual knowledge (clusters of schemata). A question that Levinson does not address adequately concerns which traditions of music should be studied to develop cultural literacy. His example, Bruckner and the classical Western tradition of music, suggests an answer, but much more needs to be said. Giving priority to the study of mainstream traditions has some benefits that he does not mention. It sensitizes learners to the presence of continuity as well as change in the history of an art and to the fact that continuities of thought and feeling are by far the greater part of the story. Science, in contrast, finds it easier to disengage itself from its past once theories are falsified. But traditional works of art cannot be falsified and may continue to serve as sources of fresh experience.

Patti P. Gillespie's "Theater Education and Hirsch's Contextualism" reveals a number of things: an uncommonly correct understanding of Hirsch; some illuminating discussion of the contexts of theater; and the discovery of some unacceptable consequences of Hirsch's notion of cultural literacy if strictly and narrowly interpreted.[9] For example, she points out that if schools teach only Hirsch's definition of cultural literacy, practically no attention would be paid to the dramatic or aesthetic features of theater performances. After a brief synopsis of the history of theater education in the United States (a context all teachers of theater should be acquainted with if they are to understand the confusion that plagues their field), Gillespie, like Sparshott and Levinson, turns her attention to the intensive curriculum.

She first observes that in many respects contemporary theater education is a perfect illustration of what Hirsch finds wrong with American education. Theater education is fragmented and discontinuous (i.e., nonsequential), oriented toward fostering personal and social skills, and inattentive to history and the major works of the Western cultural heritage (primarily popular American plays are performed in schools). Consequently, learners are denied opportunities to develop an appreciation of serious theater. Theorists of theater education ought, therefore, to examine closely what they are doing, and contextualist theory, properly conceived, would help them do that.

As a contextual critic, Gillespie enumerates some of the contexts that should be taken into account. These contexts would disclose those features of a performance that the people responsible for the performance themselves have to take into account. In this respect, Gillespie gives her discussion a slightly different twist. After noting the varieties, strengths, and limitations of formalist and contextualist criticism, she writes that contextualist criticism, when properly applied to performance (theater) in contrast to a literary text (drama), will encompass the following considerations. First there is the contextual sense of theater that design artists must bring to their creation of a suitable environment for actors, which includes knowledge of plays, set-making, and the control of lighting. Then there is the contextual sense that actors and directors need not only to interpret the meanings of texts but also to estimate their likely reception by audiences. The final interpretation may be an amalgam of imagining both the play in its original context, including its intended effect on the audiences of its time, and how contemporary circumstances affect the play. Again, it seems as if we are being overwhelmed with contextual considerations; still, there is more. Audiences too must be understood contextually, for example, with respect to what they are likely or unlikely to know about performances.

Gillespie brings all of this together when she observes, "If, as Hirsch claims, learning to read straightforward discursive prose requires cultural literacy, then 'reading' a polysemous theatrical 'text' will require a considerably more sophisticated level of cultural literacy. The more complex the play, the greater the 'literacy' required of those wishing to experience it; the greater the 'literacy' of an audience, the fuller their appreciation of performance." Actually, argues Gillespie, theater people have been speaking "Hirsch" all their lives; the rub is that now they do so before increasingly illiterate audiences. "We will soon be doing polysemous works for audiences increasingly unable to understand monosemous ones" (43). The imperative is to cultivate cultural literacy in its broad sense. To do so only in its narrow sense would be to withhold from learners opportunities to experience the import and powers of theater performances and be exposed to the capacity for teaching that is inherent in dramatic form.

Unlike some versions of contextualist criticism, to be discussed later, Gillespie favors acceptance of both formalist and contextual criticism because she does not want to sacrifice the aesthetic values of theater to wholly contextual considerations. She has no doubt that giving more attention to context in criticism could improve an understanding of theater, especially relations among text, actors, and audiences, but doing so could also, perhaps paradoxically, refocus attention on form: "A formal criticism, revised to take as its subject the *performed* play, would make possible . . . an equal status for formal and contextual criticism, to the enrichment of both" (44).

Marcia Muelder Eaton, who is a philosopher of art and interested in arts education, accents Levinson's emphasis on developing musical literacy within traditions and Gillespie's interest in a type of contextual criticism that honors both aesthetic experience and institutional considerations, hence her topic: "Context, Criticism, and Art Education:

Putting Meaning into the Life of Sisyphus."[10] Like all competent philosophers, Eaton uses a method of discussing contextualism that is as instructive as her conclusions are interesting.

A contextualist herself, Eaton first asserts that historical and critical considerations are important for an understanding of aesthetic objects and experiences and that art education is deservedly part of schooling because it contributes to the educational objective of providing for a meaningful life. But because people are willing to call so many disparate and astonishing things art (Eaton's example is cut-up parts of a slaughtered horse that were displayed in jars in a museum in Copenhagen), she feels that a definition of art is necessary. If aesthetics (the philosophy of art) cannot or will not tackle such problems, then its practice is limited to purely theoretical speculation, a situation for which Eaton is unwilling to settle.

Believing that an artwork is an artifact that has had artwork status conferred on it through the authority of someone in the established art world, Eaton reflects on the origin and status of this authority and the conditions that had to exist to make the conferral successful. This, in turn, leads her to consider how people talk about art, but that does not prove conclusive in determining what makes art actually be art. Talk about art tends to be about form, content, and context, but so does talk about many other things. This prompts a second question concerning *why* people talk about certain things and not others. Perhaps it is the goal of a discussion and not its content that counts, for this aim seems to be to bring viewers to the perception of aspects of artworks that they might have missed otherwise. Eaton thus entertains the possibility that "X is a work of art if and only if X is discussed in such a way that information about the history of production of X brings the audience to attend to features considered worthy of attention in aesthetic traditions" (100). Artifacts that are not discussed thoroughly and attentively do not become artworks because no one considers them worthy of attention.

Among the concepts featured in Eaton's definition, the most important are the concepts of aesthetic experience and tradition. Unlike a number of theorists in aesthetics (and arts education), Eaton thinks the idea of aesthetic experience is worth preserving because it manifests a characteristic delight in the aesthetic features of objects: "An aesthetic feature is an intrinsic feature traditionally considered worth attention, i.e., worthy of perception and/or reflection" (100). To be sure, Eaton acknowledges that "delight" may not appear to be the right word to capture the nature of an experience or the enjoyment of certain intrinsic qualities, for example those associated with the gratification derived from menacing and tragic artworks. But there are degrees of delight, one of which Eaton calls "deep delight."

By "tradition" Eaton implies "forms of life," a term borrowed from Wittgenstein, and she exploits it for its historical connotations:

> Forms of life are interests, goals, activities, values, rituals, institutions, etc., that communities share. They develop and are learned and passed on by way of language. I prefer the term "tradition" to "form of life" because it connotes something that I think is essential, namely, history and historical context. Values and interests are enmeshed in language which comes to us with a history. This is not to say that traditions are stable or static. As individuals and their environments alter, so does what they do and what matters to them, and this is reflected by changes in language systems. But change does not occur overnight. Meanings must change gradually or communication would be impossible. (101)

All of this is compatible with Hirsch's thinking, as is Eaton's talk about a macroculture and the microcultures it subsumes. The notion that comes closest to her use of "tradition" is that of family traditions; she conceives of traditions as belonging not only to mainstream culture but also to its subcultures. She does not, however, appear to see their relations as one of dominance (Western, male) and subordination in the manner favored by feminist critics. Each tradition identifies certain artifacts as artworks and does so through the way its members either talk about or treat these objects. Because traditions overlap, one must understand other traditions in order to better understand one's own.

Having emphasized how necessary the historical knowledge of tradition is for understanding the form of life known as art, Eaton sets out her theory of criticism. (She thinks a theory of criticism essential for arts education and therefore looks favorably upon the notion of discipline-based art education, an idea that takes art history, criticism, aesthetics, and artistic creation to be important contexts for understanding art.) Assuming that the assessment of artistic worth and aesthetic value is central to critical activity, Eaton believes that the difference between good art and bad lies in the capacity of the former, whatever its tradition, to demand and repay sustained attention. "Bad art is mindless and dulls the senses; good art is mindful and stimulates the senses" (103)—rather like the different effects implied by the terms *anaesthetic* and *aesthetic*. But why would people subject themselves to the demands of disciplined, sustained attention? The reason is the promise that if people develop their capacity for contemplation to a sufficiently high level, life will be more enjoyable and meaningful. They will find greater delight in it.

The rest of Eaton's discussion emphasizes the urgency of inviting learners into worlds of worthwhile, intrinsically interesting qualities, and of doing so in ways that take account of individual ages, backgrounds, interests, and developmental levels. Respect for learners as persons capable of transcending their current interests and expectations is also important. Good art respects the intelligence and capabilities of its audience and asks much of them, whereas bad art does neither. How can teachers induce young people to prefer better to poorer art? Consistent with her theory, Eaton recommends providing them with a tradition and then introducing them to other traditions from which they can also learn. Which traditions should schools provide and introduce?

Eaton rejects the melting pot theory of assimilation taken for granted by the schools she attended in Illinois. Yet she is aware that a loss of its traditions can have serious consequences for a society. She points out that the cultural revolution in China was propelled in part by an ignorance of traditions, one manifestation of which was the Red Guard's total lack of aesthetic sensitivity. To counteract such cultural ignorance, one must start somewhere, and Hirsch is credited for having made some concrete choices. Eaton's own teaching draws on the traditions of Western philosophy and echoes Hirsch's views on cultural literacy: One must know the ways of the dominant culture (its language and traditions, for example) not only to participate in it effectively but also to change it.

Eaton admits the difficulty of determining the amount of knowledge needed about a topic before going on to something else, for example, how much about Renaissance perspective before studying Cézanne's conception of space, or about Western culture before turning to non-Western cultures? She does stress that it takes time to learn a culture's language and traditions and that it makes sense to concentrate on the best or aesthetically superior—a belief that flies in the face of contemporary opinion that would regard such a view as elitist and undemocratic. Yet Eaton's position stems from her definition of art and the aesthetic, which once again proves the value of having a theory of art and aesthetic experience that can be brought to bear on questions regarding aesthetically better work. Eaton thinks that Vermeer is aesthetically better than Norman Rockwell, a judgment that provides a clue to others she would make.

The test of the better is always whether sustained attention to a work yields more delight (in Eaton's sense) than attention to another work. This is not to deny that aesthetically less interesting work may occasionally be the object of instruction, but it is not assumed that such work will engender the same degree of delight that aesthetically better works do. True, what sustains attention and engenders delight is always an empirical question, but we are not likely to go wrong too often if we stick with what has been traditionally valued within certain cultures. Of course, there is also the problem of the worthiness of certain traditions as a whole. "Not all traditions," writes Eaton, "are equally good, equally deserving of attention or respect" (110). One criterion of selection might be whether developing individual capacity to sustain interest in worthwhile aesthetic features is considered important. Far from thwarting human aspirations, such capacity liberates people from unnecessary restraints in order to challenge them to think and feel for themselves — which, in the vernacular of the day, is to empower them.

There are two points on which Eaton may seem at odds with Hirsch. First, her rejection of the melting pot model of social integration may suggest that she is less concerned than Hirsch with a national literate language and culture, but this possibility is countered by her qualified acceptance of the need to acquaint people with mainstream culture, language, schemata, and values. Second, her emphasis on experiencing the intrinsic features of aesthetically worthwhile objects would seem to contradict Hirsch's instrumentalism and his skeptical view of theories of intrinsic value. But Eaton sees art education as being instrumental in both a personal and a societal sense. It makes an important contribution to the meaningfulness of life by lightening the Sisyphusian burdens of human existence. Aesthetic experiences of art do this by animating the mind and feelings; they help individuals to a fuller realization of their potentialities and are constrained only by society's ethical norms. Furthermore, an art education united through the study and appreciation of quality and excellence, of the aesthetically better, contributes not only to the quality of personal life but also, indirectly, to the quality of public life. A society committed to the pursuit of aesthetic excellence is one whose members will cast a critical eye on the poorly conceived and the shabbily crafted and, by insisting on artistic value, raise the general level of cultural creativeness.

Thus far I have surveyed essays that, in a general way, address the topic of what it means to be culturally literate about the arts. This concern was reflected in Hirsch's minimal conception of the vocabulary of a national literate culture; in Sparshott's sense of what it is to take an art stance toward something and the specific knowledge required for understanding and appreciating dance; in Levinson's extended idea of cultural literacy, for example, his prescriptions for understanding music within a tradition and for the acquisition of comprehending listening abilities; in Gillespie's broad interpretation of theater literacy that distinguishes between a play as a text and a play as performed and differentiates the contextual literacies presupposed by various segments of the theater complex (designers, actors, directors, and audiences); and in Eaton's understanding of contextualism that emphasizes the role of traditions in the aesthetic experience of artworks, a type of experience that centers on the intrinsic features of things that have traditionally been considered worthwhile and thus provides a basis for recognizing aesthetically better artworks. Yet there is more to be mined from the contributions to *Cultural Literacy and Arts Education*, particularly on the general issue of contextual knowledge, in particular on its relation to art and the teaching of art.

One good example of how the misuse of contextual knowledge can obscure the character of a work is contained in Ronald Berman's "Cultural History and Cultural Materialism," which is essentially a critique of cultural materialism as an interpretive schema favored by Marxist critics.[11] Berman, a Shakespearian scholar and teacher of literature, shows how lack of concrete, historical knowledge, a faulty psychology, and excessively reductionist assumptions can put the worst possible face on Shakespeare's plays.

Berman argues that instead of researching the past in order to establish the appropriate environment for a literary work, cultural materialists tend to supply a ready-made context and force the work to accommodate itself to it, a Procrustean procedure that can leave a work of art distorted almost beyond recognition. And the reasons for such distortion are not difficult to understand. Cultural materialism is an adversarial mode of criticism that always requires literature to serve some external end, denying it any independent existence. It further holds that literature not only inevitably criticizes life but also that it must always cast its critique in political categories. Plays and other texts are "essentially, frozen examples of political relationships" (117). Because these political relationships are understood to involve offenses by the state against sex, race, and class, they produce victims. A framework of interpretation that prominently features acts of victimization perpetrated by state oppression and reenacted in relationships among individuals—the characters in a play, for example—is projected onto a literary text. Those aspects of works that cannot be brought into conformity with the interpretive perspective are discounted. Neither can any counterevidence be forthcoming from the work or from its actual historical context.

Disregard for historical and literary evidence, combined with intolerance toward dissenting interpretations, severely damages the credibility of cultural materialists. Why, asks Berman, should there be this inordinate concern to expose purported oppression and victimization? The most likely explanation is that cultural materialists take interest in literature only insofar as it can be used as a tool to delegitimize the modern state. This makes the interpretation of all literature part of a political program. Above all, the central weakness of cultural materialism is its deficiency in historical knowledge and its indifference to the aesthetic values of art. Berman illustrates these inadequacies in his analysis of *King Lear*, *Macbeth*, and Shakespeare's historical plays, in all of which the evidence of the work and an accurate knowledge of history provide evidence contrary to the interpretations laid on by cultural materialists.

Berman warns against the abstractness of ideological thinking; he expresses the same sort of caution that Trilling did at midcentury in his sympathetic critique of the liberal imagination. The tendency to construe events in terms of their social and material conditions and to see everything permeated by power relations is a case in point. In such a restrictive perspective, the potencies of ideas and the human will to effect change are nullified and the role of human biology misunderstood. Rejecting complex, multifactor explanations of human reality, cultural materialists (Marxists in general) falsify reality on behalf of an intractable and dogmatic doctrine. It is single-minded criticism of the kind practiced by Aronowitz and Giroux (chapter 3). The function of such criticism is to eradicate dissent. "The critic," observes Berman, "will tell us what to think—and he devoutly hopes to be empowered by some agency which will prohibit the teaching of evil ideas and protect the rights of good causes. It is a Marxist idyll: asserting virtue by force" (120). I add that we know it today as the enforcement of politically correct thinking.

Borrowing from Freud, Berman says human guilt and the aggressiveness inherent in human relationships have something to do with the strong, peculiar hostility toward civilization, but so does the institution of education:

> The educational world makes false demands of the real world. It sees the world of politics and economics as if it were far simpler than it actually is. And it resents having to come to terms with it. Under a "false psychological orientation, education is behaving as though one were to equip people starting on a Polar expedition with summer clothing and maps of the Italian Lakes." In this book [*Civilization and Its Discontents*] Freud's great concern was that the complexities of reality would be disguised by the demands of the ego—that "ethics" and "virtue" would be invoked as an act of aggression against culture. (120)

In short, it is paranoia to disavow the influence of human will and biology and see power relations everywhere. It is naive to think that if ideas and institutions were perfected, people would no longer be unhappy or resentful. Nevertheless, cultural materialists and determinists continue to stress the ultimate potency of material conditions and social relations for shaping reality.

In "The Visual Arts and Cultural Literacy," John Richardson endorses Hirsch's thesis that cultural literacy may consist of little more than superficial understanding, a point that Richardson himself (who is knowledgeable in a number of fields, including art, art history, design, and science) made in the preface to his introductory text *Art: The Way It Is*. There he said that he could do no more than "gloss surfaces for there are basic difficulties in dealing with a thing so all-encompassing as art." [12] This is true especially of visual art, where language has to be strained to accommodate the concept of "visual literacy." Unlike the writers of some of the other essays discussed so far, Richardson does not deal systematically with contextual knowledge, but conveys his ideas through illuminating observations and entertaining anecdotes. Indeed, he is one of the few writers about art and education today who has a genuine wit and capacity for turning a phrase.

Richardson tells the story of how early in his career he was challenged to formulate an on-the-spot definition of a good general education. He replied by saying that such a program might well produce graduates who would not embarrass themselves at cocktail parties in Manhattan or Belgravia (precisely what Gombrich said the character in the Agatha Christie novel did). Or, we might say, a little cultural knowledge might enable them to "come and go talking of Michelangelo," the lines of T. S. Eliot that Hirsch chose as the epigraph for his essay in *Cultural Literacy and Arts Education*. Recalling some findings of an experimental curriculum in design education in which he was involved, Richardson wonders whether a program of general education might also be effective in cultivating some genuinely liberal values in college youth, at least to the extent that they might hesitate to enter a life devoted solely to crass materialism.

Richardson reflects not only on the enabling powers but also on the shortcomings of items of knowledge that might qualify as cultural literacy. As an example of the former, he refers to the Lisbon earthquake of 1755 (not on Hirsch's list). It is not necessary to memorize the date or recall the historical details of this horrific event to grasp its consequences, not least for the art of the eighteenth century and the work of Giovanni Battista Piranesi. Bits of information about events like the Lisbon earthquake, observes Richardson, provide a toehold for a further ascent up the ladder of knowledge. Yet superficial contextual knowledge can also mislead, as Richardson points out in noting Hirsch's dictionary entry for John Constable. Although it may count for something to recognize Constable as a British painter and not mistake him for an American sculptor,

> merely to know that John Constable is "an English landscape painter of the late eighteenth and early nineteenth centuries, known for pastoral scenes," is to be aware of a bit that is correct and a little that is, perhaps, misleading—particularly when given the literary connotations of the term "pastoral," with its generally bucolic overtones. Certainly, John Constable was in love with the English countryside in somewhat the same way as his friend William Wordsworth was, but what characterizes his painting style is the particular approach he made toward the problem of *rendering* nature, and it is not very informative to speak of his works in terms of subject matter. (63)

What we might call the aesthetic literacy of the viewer of art should thus include knowing what is essential about a work in a particular style

or from a particular period. Richardson remarks that when one is dealing with the romantics and the realists of the nineteenth century certain
considerations become more relevant than others. For all that can be
said about the importance of the subject matter of a romantic or realistic work, "it is the sheer appearance of the work that is the basis of its
importance" (64). In one respect, Richardson says that this is true of all
visual art, a point he elaborates in order to establish the distinctiveness
of image art.

Richardson makes several other observations about cultural literacy.
People should probably know something about the life of art in an essentially hierarchical, capitalistic, and elitist social system whose social arrangements he does not regard as inherently racist, sexist, or inhuman,
nor even, given the commitment to social welfare policies, capitalistic
in a strict sense. And he further believes, as do Hirsch and many others,
that such a society "demands for its dynamic a culturally literate group
to operate it in a decently just and responsible way" (67). Contrary to
writers like Aronowitz and Giroux, Richardson acknowledges the necessity to tolerate some things we do not like while leaving open the
possibility for social reform. With a sense of curiosity and humor, and
perhaps a little self-doubt, Richardson, like several other readers, had
fun skimming through the entries on Hirsch's list.

The potency for generating wider insights that Richardson ascribed to
some elementary knowledge about the Lisbon earthquake may also belong to superficial acquaintance with the "iconoclastic controversy" (not
on "the list"). As Clifton Olds points out in "Jan Gossaert's *St. Luke
Painting the Virgin:* A Renaissance Artist's Cultural Literacy," this historical and cultural event significantly influenced the style and content
of painting.[13] Like Richardson, Olds has some qualms about using the
term *literacy* to describe a painter's intuitive comprehension of cultural
patterns and presences because in its standard meaning "literacy" implies knowledge expressed in words. Works of visual art are images that
must always be interpreted (when they lend themselves to interpretation) as speculative and provisional because of the limitations inherent
in verbal translations of nonverbal messages.

Olds makes the iconoclastic controversy central to his discussion of
Gossaert's *St. Luke* painting. It was inevitable that this dispute would
have an impact on the visual arts of the time because one side interpreted the commandments of the Old Testament God as proscribing the
making of images, in effect, questioning the very legitimacy of painting.

On the other hand, the Bible also mentions St. Luke's having made a picture of the Virgin, and he is consequently credited with having been the first Christian artist. Painters saw to it that images of the saint painting the Virgin adorned their guildhalls so as to legitimize their art.

The particular form the iconoclastic controversy took in the Netherlands during the sixteenth century is especially important for understanding Gossaert's *St. Luke*. The work, writes Olds, "must certainly be considered the work of an artist working in a Catholic world and familiar with the traditional defense of religious imagery. It is in that light that one must consider the iconographic peculiarities of the work" (93). The ability to interpret the iconographic peculiarities of this painting defines not only Gossaert's cultural literacy but also that of his contemporaries, whom he counted on to construe his work properly. Today this ability—the ability to discern which aspects of the depicted scene are departures from the traditional rendering and are in all likelihood specific responses to the renewed threat of iconoclasm—would have to become part of the contextual framework of any viewer wishing to understand the painting at a deeper rather than at a superficial level. "Gossaert's painting," concludes Olds, "becomes a powerful defense of the artist, whose gifts are obviously God-given, whose hand is guided by an agent of the Lord, whose vision is truly visionary, whose profession can boast of a saintly Evangelist, and whose obedience to Mosaic law does not preclude the creation of works of art. As a response to those who preached the abolition of religious imagery, it makes an argument that would echo throughout the years of the Counter-Reformation" (94).

Hirsch's *Dictionary* includes only two references in the section on religion to the biblical figure of Luke, but of course none to "St. Luke Painting the Virgin" as a subject of many paintings. Perhaps it is not necessary for literate Americans to know about the latter, but after reading Olds one suspects that the iconoclastic controversy should be in Hirsch's lexicon.

Olds says nothing about the artistic excellence or aesthetic values of the *St. Luke*. He limits himself to only one perspective of the art stance; presumably, he takes the other two for granted. Still, his interpretation is an excellent example of how contextual knowledge can reveal the character of an artwork.

In "Literature, Education, and Cultural Literacy," Walter Clark, Jr., a professor of English and literature as well as a poet, places the discussion of cultural literacy in the context of teacher education.[14] What do future teachers need to know in order to be culturally literate? In setting out some of his beliefs, Clark first sketches the background he brings to a reading of Hirsch. Although he is wary of proposals that stress merely amassing information (recalling Whitehead's dictum that "knowledge doesn't keep any better than fish"), Clark takes Hirsch's recommendations seriously. Like Hirsch, he thinks that certain kinds of knowledge are needed more than other kinds, that a shared body of knowledge contributes to effective communication, that too often an unnecessary separation exists between learning and living, and that the lack of opportunity to study common materials sacrifices the important sort of learning that accrues when students discuss and debate such materials outside the classroom.

Looking over the literature entries on Hirsch's list, Clark wonders not only how many youngsters are likely to have encountered them before school attendance and whether people still read aloud to young children, but also whether in a metropolitan and electronic age the Mother Goose rhymes, which reflect an agrarian era, should still receive as much attention as Hirsch accords them or whether "Sesame Street" should also be consulted for common material. He further speculates about the ways in which people may have come into possession of the items on the list and reminisces about his own acquisition of some. He recalls acquiring items seemingly without much understanding, whereas others came to him as part of a contextual web of information that required greater comprehension. Taking a metaphor from economics, Clark suggests that "perhaps we can see Hirsch as urging the importance of providing the learner with the basic currency of cultural exchange at an early stage in his or her intellectual development. He wants to see a common currency of information in general possession and circulation. He is convinced the resultant activity will lead to an increase in currency, and also to increased intellectual 'backing' " (52).

After an estimation of how many of the literature items would be acquired, through what agency, and at what times in the learner's life, Clark concludes that the responsibility for the development of cultural literacy falls not only to the schools (Hirsch's primary locus for development) but also to parents, television, and newspapers—to all the groups and institutions in society that have some educational responsibilities, including colleges and teacher-preparation programs. Prospective teachers might be tested on the items on the list, but their grasp of them should go beyond simple recognition. Clark realizes that Hirsch, whose view of information is sophisticated, insists on its relevant contextualization. Recalling the iceberg analogy used to explain the relation between explicit and tacit knowledge, Clark writes:

> The body of the information iceberg must be dealt with as well as the tip. Not only does the tip exist for the sake of the body, if we accept Hirsch's use of reading schemata, but acquisition of the body is the best assurance that the student will retain the tip, as Whitehead's remark about knowledge and fish suggests. The implications for transmission of the list seem fairly clear. The set of explicit meanings of its items constitute the tips of icebergs on which each learner is to "grow" his own substratum. The implications for the preparation of teachers would seem to be equally clear. The teacher cannot escape responsibility for this process and therefore, to the extent possible, must have a substrate of his own. Another way to put this is that the teacher should be able to go below water line with most items on the list, and to go considerably below water line with some items, including not only the teacher's area of academic specialty but also a random sprinkling of other items. Finally, both teachers and teacher training programs still have to confront the issues implicit in Hirsch's reference to "relevant information." (53–54)

Clark concludes with observations on the uses of Hirsch's *Cultural Literacy* in teacher preparation programs. So far as literature teachers are concerned, they should have read everything on Hirsch's list and much more; have some proficiency in a foreign language so as to appreciate the problems of translation; have read drama and worked in theater (to recall Gillespie's distinction) to be able to help students with the mounting of plays; have read some of the novels on Hirsch's list more closely; and have done a lot of writing. But they should also have some understanding of schema theory and the nature of knowledge and its acquisition. Their reading of Hirsch should be further extended by some historical and sociological understanding of literacy and its current status. What, for example, were the conditions that led to Hirsch's project, and how does one assess his sociology of knowledge? Although Clark believes that *Cultural Literacy* should be part of every English teacher's cultural knowledge, he also thinks that the best preparation for teaching the items on Hirsch's list is a general, liberal education.

His benign skepticism notwithstanding, Clark clearly appreciates the need for and uses of Hirsch's notion of cultural literacy. Clark's broad knowledge and experience and his concern for literature, learning, and teacher education are all refreshing and counter many of Hirsch's critics. To be sure there is always, as Dewey and other educational reformers came to understand only too well, the danger that worthwhile ideas may suffer the fate of misinterpretation and oversimplification. "All too easily," writes Clark, "in the hands of uninspired time servers, it could become a mechanical albatross to hang around the necks of uncomprehending students" (56). Yet a broad, liberal education, greater concern for teaching, and a better understanding of the nature of knowledge and its acquisition are hedges against incoherence and irrelevance. Clark asks whether colleges, English departments, and teacher-preparation programs are doing all they should in these respects.

In "Aesthetic Literacy: The Psychological Context," Michael J. Parsons, an educational theorist with a strong interest in visual arts education, puts the question of cultural literacy in terms of the aesthetic literacy required to understand art and what is involved in developing it.[15] Parsons begins with Hirsch's discussion of the extensive and intensive curriculums and the relations between the two, being primarily interested in what should determine the character of the intensive curriculum of the secondary years of schooling. He addresses this question by appealing to the insights of developmental psychology and contemporary aesthetic theory.

Developmental psychology counsels that before introducing adult ways of understanding and appreciating art, the comprehensions adolescents bring with them to their aesthetic encounters should first be ascertained. What, in other words, is the character of their interpretive schemata? I think Parsons misreads Hirsch when he ascribes to him the belief that the interpretive frameworks of the intensive curriculum are superficial and easily acquired. Indeed, Hirsch would agree with Parsons that, in contrast to the knowledge to be conveyed in the extensive curriculum, the concepts of the intensive curriculum are more complex and systematically arranged. Yet Parsons agrees that interpretive schemata for art are conditioned by contextual knowledge, notably by a sense of an art world that presupposes some knowledge of art's history and its theory. To use terms introduced earlier, appropriate interpretive schemata presuppose the ability to take an art stance toward certain artifacts. Parsons rightly points out that because of the diverse sources of the knowledge, values, and attitudes that comprise them, interpretive schemata may not be identified and taught easily.

To try to detect the character of the interpretative schemata that young persons bring to their perceptions of art works, Parsons, over a period of ten years, examined people's responses to a number of re-productions. The result of his investigation was the tentative identifi-cation of five stages of aesthetic growth—favoritism, beauty and real-ism, expressiveness, style and form, and autonomy—each of which he understands not in terms of age so much as in conceptual finesse. What differentiates each stage is a person's relative success in taking an art stance toward an artifact. The mistakes that people make in respond-ing to artworks indicate the points at which to aim specific instruction. This echoes Hirsch's admonition that framers of the intensive curricu-lum must be as explicit as those who design the extensive curriculum. To illustrate his point, Parsons discusses what would be involved in teach-ing about the work of an artist in a particular style, for example, Renoir in the impressionist style. Assuming that understanding such a style pre-supposes a sense of history, Parsons recounts the responses of different people in order to reveal how such a sense informs their reactions, what he calls an excursus into the natural history of the understanding of a style. I think that the implications of Parson's discussion of aesthetic growth are consistent with Hirsch's views: The teaching of aesthetic skills needs to be combined with particular information. There is no other way to ensure comprehension of a historical style. For further in-formation about Parsons's research, his *How We Understand Art* can be consulted.[16]

David Elliott's "Music as Culture: Toward a Multicultural Concept of Arts Education" is flawed by so profound a misunderstanding of Hirsch's intentions that the essay might have been included in the discussion in chapter 3.[17] Elliott finds Hirsch's emphasis on the learning of a national literate language too limiting because he thinks it subordinates the arts to the "fine arts" and relegates multicultural education to a secondary status. Like so many of the critiques of Hirsch, Elliott's response is viti-ated by his failure to have read Hirsch carefully and completely. Elliott, too, shows a tendency to ascribe to the whole of the curriculum what Hirsch specifies for only one part of it. And he further uses Hirsch as an occasion to set out his own multicultural concept of music educa-tion which, he thinks, might be applicable to arts education in general.

Accordingly, Elliott provides definitions of culture, multiculturalism, music, and music education as multicultural education.

Elliott's definition of culture from an anthropological point of view, his distinctions between macroculture and microculture, and the importance he attaches to people's participation in culture are all fine except that, once more, much of it is not, as he seems to think, a criticism of Hirsch. Once it is realized that much of what Elliott wants can be carried out in what Hirsch calls the intensive curriculum of the secondary years, Elliott's apprehensions have less foundation.

Elliott understands the term *multiculturalism* to have normative rather than descriptive force; it implies an effective commitment to cultural pluralism and diversity as a basis for organizing a viable system of social organization. This much may be accepted. But from the fact that the United States is a pluralistic democratic society currently experiencing difficulties in addressing the grievances of many different groups it does not follow that Hirsch's agenda is undemocratic. He does not demand cultural uniformity, nor is he bent on curtailing liberty or disenfranchising people. On the contrary, it is precisely Hirsch's aim to make a democratic society more democratic by enabling people to participate as fully as possible in the life of society. It is a basic misunderstanding of Hirsch's argument that causes Elliott to say so many peculiar things, for example that Hirsch does not realize that inequality exists in American schooling or that certain institutions exert excessive power. Hirsch is hardly that naive. He is merely saying that a higher level of literacy than that which now obtains will be necessary to effect social change in morally acceptable ways and directions. To speak, therefore, of Hirsch's "grim reductionism" is to have misread him. There is nothing grim or limiting in wanting to empower people to play a more effective role in culture. Because Elliott's heart is the right place and his intentions honorable, it is unfortunate that he felt the need to caricature Hirsch, who, properly understood, could be his ally.

Elliott's misunderstanding of Hirsch continues in his discussion of music. Hirsch could accept, I think, most of the sensible things Elliott says about music but would remind him that *Cultural Literacy* is concerned with only a partial knowledge of music which it is, once more, the task of the extensive curriculum to convey. That leaves quite a lot for the intensive curriculum to do. Indeed, Elliott is much more interesting when he is talks about what he knows best, the musical complex. His fourfold schema for understanding music (a doer, a doing, something done, and a context in which the doing is done) is helpful and recalls the various things that bear on musical understanding. Indeed, there is little to criticize in his context-dependent explanation of music. His likening of his concept of culture to the reality of music is also acceptable in the sense in which he understands it. It is not surprising, for example, that the dynamics of a music world should exhibit relationships similar to those of the larger culture's.

Elliott further quotes some eminently sound passages from the writings of Israel Scheffler. For example, on the idea of a living tradition Scheffler writes, "To view past works . . . as given and unique objects rather than as incarnations of process is to close off the traditions of effort from which they emerged. It is to bring these traditions to a full stop. Viewing such works as embodiments of purpose, style, and form revivifies and extends the force of these traditions in the present, giving hope to creative impulses now and in the future." [18]

That is worth saying and emphasizes a point made in Sparshott's discussion of dance. And Elliott's discussion of learning to listen to a historical style recalls Levinson's, Eaton's, and Parsons's remarks about learning to appreciate something within a tradition. Pedagogical value also resides in Elliott's "three-eared" construal of musical experience. That is, "One ear processes a given pattern of sounds as tones in and of themselves (inherent meaning); one ear processes sounds as belonging to a web of socially defined (delineated or categorical) meanings ('tones for this person?'); and one ear merges the sound heard in these two ways to provide one's 'musical experience' or not" (159–60). Moreover, the study of alternatives, which Elliott endorses strongly, is consistent with a traditional goal of humanistic education, for it counteracts narrowness and cautions against the tendency to impose the musical standards and expectations of one culture on another.

Elliott's discussion, borrowing from Richard Pratte, of six approaches to multicultural education (assimilationist, amalgamationist, open society, ethnic, modified, and dynamic) helps clarify the strengths and weaknesses of each.[19] His preference is for what Pratte calls a dynamic multiculturalism that "emphasizes the need to convert subgroup affiliation into a community of interest through a shared commitment to a common purpose" (163). I assume that the common purpose referred to is the knowledge of self and its relation to others and to culture (i.e., humanistic knowledge). But because Elliott assigns to music education the task of applying a critical perspective to a broad range of musical cultures, I am not certain how he intends to handle the problem of selecting curriculum content. Teaching people to listen comprehendingly in one musical tradition takes a good deal of time, and when it is extended to a number of traditions the result is bound to be less than wholly successful; it would also constitute only one part of a program of general education.

Elliott's view of multiculturalism also seems to necessitate conveying encyclopedic knowledge about numerous different cultures and their music. But if, to make things more manageable, one musical tradition—say, the Western musical tradition, which would be a reasonable choice in view of the influence of this tradition on American culture—is given precedence and supplemented by the music of one or two other cultures, African or Asian perhaps, then it seems misleading to speak of music as multicultural education. Music education with a multicultural dimension would appear to be a more accurate name. Nothing Elliott says, however, really amounts to a strong argument against Hirsch's limited recommendations.

The essays from *Cultural Literacy and Arts Education* discussed in this chapter are notable for the ways they can help readers understand cultural literacy in the arts as a species of cultural literacy in Hirsch's sense, and the role of contextual knowledge, comprised of items of information like those on Hirsch's list, in the teaching and learning of art. "Context" and "contextual knowledge" have been understood loosely as the circumstances surrounding artworks and the background knowledge brought to the experience of them.

CHAPTER FIVE

The Question
of Multiculturalism

IN A GLOBAL CONTEXT, the term *multiculturalism in arts education* suggests the study of the arts of all civilizations, Western and non-Western. In the national context of the United States, it usually implies that greater attention should be paid to the cultural expressions of ethnic and minority groups. But if this were all that multiculturalism denoted there would be no major issue, for increasingly volumes on the history of art are histories of world art, and school textbooks are being rewritten to reflect the contributions to American life of groups previously given little or no consideration. What makes multiculturalism a matter for serious concern is its transformation into an extreme ideology whose purpose is to undermine the significance of Western civilization by claiming that Western traditions, owing to their purported racism, sexism, and elitism, are the cause of most of our modern problems. An increasing number of writers now believe that considerations of ethnic origin, class, and gender are more important in making policy decisions for art education than the historical influence or artistic excellence of works of art. As Roger Kimball, an astute observer of current trends, puts matters,

> Implicit in the politicizing mandate of multiculturalism is an attack on the idea of a common culture, the idea that, despite our many differences, we hold in common an intellectual, artistic, and moral legacy, descending largely from the Greeks and the Bible, supple-

mented and modified over the centuries by innumerable contributions from diverse hands and peoples. It is this legacy that has given us our science, our political institutions, and the monuments of artistic and cultural achievement that define us a civilization. Indeed, it is this legacy, in so far as we live up to it, that preserves us from chaos and barbarism. And it is precisely this legacy that the multiculturalist wishes to dispense with. Either he claims that the Western tradition is merely one heritage among many—and therefore that it deserves no special allegiance inside the classroom or out of it—or he denies the achievements of the West altogether.[1]

In some instances, multiculturalism and cultural pluralism are rejected in favor of promoting a cultural particularism that stresses radical difference and separatism.

But even if we reject extremist thinking, as I think we must, the idea of multicultural understanding raises several interesting and challenging questions. What, precisely, do we mean by "multiculturalism," "multicultural understanding," "multicultural education," and "multicultural arts education"? What proportion of a curriculum should be given over to multicultural aims and objectives? What kinds of methods are appropriate for studying the arts of different cultures and groups? How much knowledge and expertise are required to do so? Most of all, how can we avoid shallowness of understanding? And because, as Eaton remarked, not all cultures, or all of the features of some cultures, are worth studying, what constitutes worthwhileness, and who decides? Such things were more or less on my mind when some years ago I attempted to come to terms with the problems of cultural diversity in the arts in an international context.[2] I now assess such problems and issues in light of the current situation.

My thinking about cultural diversity was stimulated by participation in a number of world congresses of the International Society for Education through Art (INSEA), an organization whose formation was influenced by Herbert Read and whose founding president was Edwin Ziegfeld of Teachers College, Columbia University.[3] During the seventies and eighties I also spoke at various foreign universities and polytechnics in England, Australia, Canada, Holland, Italy, and Japan. I discovered not only varying degrees of seriousness in attempts to come to terms with the problems of cultural diversity but also a failure to make some necessary distinctions. Because I am not a social scientist and tend to look at things from the point of view of the humanities, I found the writings of the late Walter Kaufmann useful.

Kaufmann was a professor of philosophy at Princeton University and taught and wrote widely on the nature of philosophy, tragedy, religion, and existentialism. In *The Future of the Humanities* he addressed the crisis of the humanities in higher education and concluded that humanists must start teaching the humanities differently lest humanity itself becomes dehumanized.[4] In particular, he thought higher education should clarify and redefine the goals of the humanities and achieve consensus on appropriate methods of teaching. He was convinced, for example, that most professors and students do not know how to read a classic text; yet if the humanities neglect to engender this capacity, they have no raison-d'être.

What Kaufmann says about reading classic texts in higher education also applies to teaching an understanding of literature and the arts in the schools. The ability to read and perceive works of literature and the visual and performing arts is rarely cultivated. The principal reason often given for cultural illiteracy in the arts is the low value that schools place on teaching the arts. But another explanation is that art theorists and teachers have had the wrong priorities; for they have too long concentrated on creative and performing activities. Only recently has the field begun to show some interest in works of art as loci of aesthetic and humanistic value.

Kaufmann states that the purposes of teaching the humanities are four: the conservation and preservation of the greatest works of humanity; the teaching of vision; the development of a critical spirit; and, especially at issue, the examination of alternatives. The principal reason for studying alternatives is to foster a critical spirit that enables one to detect in alternatives what speaks for and against them and what, consequently, reinforces or contradicts one's own ideas.

Kaufmann's reflections were published just as the trend known as deconstruction was beginning to influence departments of philosophy and literature, whence it has spread to other disciplines and areas of study, including arts education. The deconstructivist attitude toward texts and its nihilistic consequences are anathema not only to Kaufmann's thinking but also to any responsible and serious theory of arts education.[5] Kaufmann seems to have deconstructivists in mind when he charges that the humanities are being dehumanized by those who no longer take seriously the critical analysis of a text's intellectual, moral, and aesthetic values. For many teachers of the humanities, "The text is secondary, the author matters scarcely at all, and what counts is the game in which the text is a mere prop—rather like a board on which one tries to make some clever moves."[6]

In "The Art of Reading" Kaufmann likens the reading of a classic text to a visit to a foreign land and to a conscious search for culture shock.[7] He distinguishes four ways of reading—exegetical, dogmatic, agnostic, and dialectical—only the last of which is a proper way to engage a text. It alone, he thinks, is consistent with the goals of the humanities. An analogy to multicultural studies suggests itself; we may speak of exegetical, dogmatic, agnostic, and dialectical ways of confronting alien cultures, the aim being to experience culture shock.

The Exegetical Reader and the Exegetical Multiculturist

Exegesis is associated with the interpretation of biblical texts and has a long and venerable history. Although Kaufmann finds fault with this method of reading, he does not deny its important function and insights. The limitation of the method is its assumption that the interpreter, the exegete, possesses the truth contained in texts and must therefore interpret and communicate it to the unknowing. Typically, exegetical interpreters first select a major text, say the Bible or *Das Kapital*, endow it with authority, and then read their own ideas into it, especially those ideas which reflect strong beliefs and emotional commitments. Consequently, exegetical readers receive their own ideas back clothed in the text's authority. But because emotional identification with the text tends to precede close reading, there is potential for biased understanding. Many people, and not only scholars, read in this fashion. Exegetical readers do not seek an alternative experience that might question their own values and beliefs, but search instead for confirmation of preconceived notions and feelings. This tendency closes off the possibility of genuine existential encounters and invites self-deception and arbitrariness. Exegetical readers insulate themselves against culture shock by playing it safe. They are like travelers who stay at the Hilton wherever they go because things there are familiar and comfortable.

The mistakes of exegetical multiculturists are similar. They endow not a text but a different culture with superior merit and authority, read their own sentiments and allegiances into it, and then receive their own outlook back, reinforced and substantiated. The next step is to instruct the uninitiated. Typically, exegetical multiculturalists extol the qualities and virtues of alien cultures in order to criticize their own. For example, in an effort to call critical attention to the adverse effects of advanced technologies on the aesthetic quality of life, exegetical multicultural-ists may highlight what appears to be the functional interdependence of the aesthetic with other aspects of living in another society, perhaps in Javanese or Balinese cultures. Conversely, technologically advanced civilizations are chastised for having institutionalized the aesthetic im-pulse in cultural organizations—museums, galleries, performing arts centers, and so forth—the selective policies of which are claimed to en-courage cultural elitism. The fact that persons of all classes derive a distinctive and important kind of experience from going to museums and attending musical performances and plays is conveniently over-looked.

Exegetical multiculturalists tend to ignore yet another possibility. Close and unbiased scrutiny of a preferred culture may reveal prac-tices and values that in good conscience cannot be endorsed, a concern that Eaton expressed. Subtle and not so subtle social and class distinc-tions may obtain within an ostensibly communitarian and collectivist society. A culture noted for its aesthetic way of life may suppress per-sonal autonomy, self-expression, and individual development. In short, exegetical visitors to foreign cultures may fail to see the whole picture. However much they may desire the integration of aesthetic and social values, exegetical multiculturalists are ill advised to denigrate cultural institutions that appear to separate art from life. It is, after all, these in-stitutions that conserve and replenish the aesthetic wealth of a culture, a wealth embodied in some of the finest creative and spiritual monuments of the human race. Francis Haskell, a British art historian, has pointed out that without museums and libraries and concert halls many of these achievements would have been lost forever. Many artifacts, moreover, have now been in art-institutional contexts longer than in their original ones and have consequently taken on a life of their own.[8]

Little more needs to be said about exegetical multiculturalists. They are familiar participants in conferences and world congresses, where they expound their presumably superior wisdom. Yet their capacity for self-deception and personal embarrassment is often as great as that of hidebound cultural chauvinists. The fact that ethnocentrism of the "my culture first and foremost" variety has now become acceptable reflects the dramatic social changes that have occurred since the early days of anthropology. Once deplored as a defect in a person's outlook, ethnocentrism is now regarded by many as something to be cultivated. Exegetical multiculturalism is educationally limiting because it subverts one of the main objectives of teaching the humanities—to help persons think critically and judge for themselves.

The Dogmatic Reader and the Dogmatic Multiculturalist

Dogmatic readers assume that their own culture is superior and that others fail to pass muster. Both they and their counterparts, the dogmatic multiculturists, avoid the experience of culture shock and the serious study of alternatives for what it can contribute to self-understanding. Their "my country right or wrong" posture resembles that of vulgar jingoists. One observes this attitude mostly in government and business leaders who believe that the world would be much better off if all "backward" nations would simply adopt the economic and technological capabilities of "advanced" ones. Such a patronizing stance is also taken by dogmatic multiculturalists toward cultures they consider backward or primitive. Because the preferences of multicultural dogmatists are grounded in flawed arguments, they are implausible and indefensible. Dogmatists in general avoid exposure to alternatives and do not seek self-illumination.

Dogmatists, moreover, almost exclusively impute the vice of cultural chauvinism to Western societies, which are accused of being smugly superior, ethnocentric, and imperialistic. Yet there is reason to believe that chauvinism is not confined to the West; even a superficial knowledge of anthropology confirms that self-interest is a well-cultivated inclination of humankind.

The Agnostic Reader and the Agnostic Multiculturalist

Agnostic readers, who embody Kaufmann's third type of attitude toward a text, avoid the principal error of exegetical and dogmatic readers, that is, the mistake of reading preconceived ideas and judgments into a text.

In this respect the agnostic attitude is preferable. Yet their lack of bias does not render agnostic readers immune to criticism. Agnostic readers assume that because they cannot possess the whole truth about something, they must suspend judgment; questions of value and assessment are not important. Yet closing themselves off to these dimensions makes it impossible for agnostic readers to have the most complete and undistorted encounter with a text. Furthermore, the neutrality of agnostic readers stems less from a desire for fairness than it does from indifference. In truth, their attention is directed elsewhere: to antiquarian, aesthetic, or microscopic interests. The antiquarian interest is like the stamp collector's; the aesthetic interest (in Kaufmann's use of the term) reflects a penchant for beauty and style, or for mere surface phenomena; and a microscopic interest focuses on a part rather than the whole—or, to use Kaufmann's example, on the specialized study not of the leech but of the leech's brain. To recall the foreign-visitor analogy, agnostic multiculturalists are like travelers who not only stay at the Hilton because everything there is familiar and comfortable but who also delight in the picture postcards and souvenirs they take home.

Now souvenir-collecting multiculturalists are at least interested in learning something about different cultures, otherwise they would not take the time to visit them. Typically, however, their haste permits only brief glimpses of things along the way, and this defeats the purpose of studying a culture for what it might contribute to self-understanding. They are prevented from experiencing culture shock and exploring alternative values by their preference for things old, rare, or merely different, for surface qualities, or for a tiny part of the whole. What is especially valuable about and relevant to a particular culture—for example, how its members view the world from a special vantage point—is not important. One's own views and preconceptions remain secure, and there is no threat to the self. For such an attitude we reserve the term *parochial*.

Agnostic multiculturalists are also easy to spot at art education conferences, the type of gathering with which I am most familiar. They are the casual, relatively disengaged participants who have collected hundreds, perhaps thousands, of children's drawings and paintings from around the globe and who thus reflect an essentially botanizing interest in children's artworks. Matters of cultural context and values are secondary, if any interest is taken in them at all. Charming as all of this can be, it hardly qualifies as genuine understanding; there is no pursuit of self-knowledge that derives from a scrutiny of difference. In truth, the information provided by agnostic multiculturalists is often so superficial that it is more misleading than educative.

The Dialectical Reader and the Dialectical Multiculturalist

Because of its association with Hegelian and Marxist analysis, or with mere scholastic cleverness, the term *dialectical* is perhaps not the best choice for what Kaufmann means. *Critical* might suffice, except that it is too vague for Kaufmann's purposes. What he wants to emphasize by using "dialectical" is a demanding and significant encounter with a text. In the context of the discussion in this chapter, this would be extended to mean a demanding and significant encounter with the arts of a different culture.

In Kaufmann's analysis, a dialectical encounter with a text has three components: the Socratic, the dialogical, and the historical-philosophical. This triad of considerations is consistent with his belief that the serious reading of a classic text is essentially a voyage in search of culture shock for the purpose of self-examination. It means nothing less than taking seriously the Socratic maxim that the unexamined life is not worth living. The dialectical reader assumes that neither the reader nor the author of a text is omniscient but that, being intelligent, they can attempt to transcend their limitations by joining in a common quest. This means that the voice of a text is addressed as a You and that the reader's goal is to view matters outside the currently existing consensuses. The resultant culture shock is a precondition for better self-understanding.

The dialogical aspect of dialectical reading consists of a conscious effort to discern the distinctive voice of a text, however much that voice may disturb, challenge, and offend one's sensibility. Dialectical reading is thus nonauthoritarian. There is no prior commitment to a text's authority nor a predisposition to make the text conform to one's own beliefs. It is through such deliberate study that consciousness is raised and clarified. By "raising consciousness" Kaufmann does not, of course, imply self-destructive experimentation with mind-damaging drugs—there is to be no celebrating with Timothy Leary—but rather "the liberation from parochialism and cultural conditioning, the freedom that is born when the awareness of a multitude of alternatives issues in the creation of new ways."[9]

The third component of dialectical reading—the historical-philosophical element—is necessary to discover the intention of a text's author. In the case of a classic text this is not easy and requires careful reading and rereading. At this point Kaufmann asks readers to envision three concentric circles.

Careful reading requires beginning with the innermost circle, the text itself and ostensibly the locus of its intention and distinctive voice. It is as if Kaufmann is endorsing the advice of Matthew Arnold, who said that the critic's task is to try to see a text as in itself it really is, with as little distortion and bias as possible. This is the courtesy, as Lionel Trilling once put it, that we extend to a text even though we know that total objectivity is unattainable because of the ways interpretive frameworks influence understanding.[10]

To seek further assistance in discerning the intention and meaning of a text, one moves beyond the innermost circle, the text itself, into the second concentric circle, where the task becomes that of relating the text to the writer's other work and career. The purpose of this inquiry is to discover the writer's spiritual personality, peculiar cast of mind, and style of thinking. One also takes note of the weight of a particular text in a writer's artistic production. Yet the serious dialectical reader does not stop with the disclosure of the writer's persona. There is still a third concentric circle to explore, and this involves the study of a writer's background, artistic development, and the views of other readers. It should be apparent not only that these three concentric circles of inquiry overlap but also that one travels back and forth among them—from text to author to background, back to author and text, and so forth.

Thus the attitude of the dialectical reader is neither presumptuous nor indifferent. It is perhaps best described as the "nervous wariness" that Irving Howe identified as Trilling's way of approaching a serious work of literature. Trilling "would circle a work with his fond, nervous wariness as if in the presence of some force, some living energy, which could not always be kept under proper control—indeed as if approaching an elemental power. The work came alive and therefore was never quite knowable, alive and therefore even threatened the very desires and values that first made us approach it." [11] This passage characterizes the spirit of the dialectical encounter more accurately than even Kaufmann's argument and goes to the heart of what he means by it.

Kaufmann believes that the best method for shedding a narrow ethnocentrism is to study texts and artworks from highly different cultures. There can be no question that this will often be helpful, but I do not think that it is always necessary. Past periods and epochs in one's own cultural heritage can serve as well; they are often as puzzling and inaccessible as alien cultures.

Consider, for example, Trilling's experience in a course he taught during the seventies on the novels of Jane Austen. He discovered that his students had great difficulty comprehending and sympathetically participating in the world in which Austen's characters lived and moved.[12] The students confined their responses to what Kaufmann calls the innermost circle of the complete act of reading, the text itself, and even there they achieved only partial understanding. They were literally at a loss to appreciate anything in the novel's outer circles, for example, the symbols and codes that governed life in Austen's time, norms that implied particular attitudes toward family relations, toward being and doing, and toward duty—all standards of conduct that readers of Austen's own time would have taken for granted. Because of his students' inability to identify with Austen's characters, Trilling had to devote considerable time to supplying relevant background information.

For Trilling's students, then, Jane Austen's early-nineteenth-century world was literally a foreign country. Although they professed an interest in reading Austen for whatever insights they might garner for their own quest for self-definition, which is consistent with dialectical reading, their limited knowledge prevented the students from fully engaging her works. Not only that; I infer from what Trilling says that the students' desire to read Austen (five years earlier, in 1968, they were demanding to read William Blake) originated in an essentially exegetical attitude. They were interested in reading their own ideas, values, and needs into Austen's works in order to receive them back invested with Austen's authority. This experience prompted Trilling to reflect on a major assumption of modern literary criticism—that one reads best by sympathetically identifying with the characters of a story and imaginatively participating in their worlds.

To gain an alternative way of understanding the people and values of a different world, Trilling turned to the writings of the anthropologist Clifford Geertz. After reading his studies of alien cultures, Trilling remarked on Geertz's method for entering into the workings of a different society. "In each case," reports Geertz, "I have tried to arrive at this most intimate of notions not by imagining myself as someone else—a rice peasant or a tribal sheik, and seeing what I thought—but by searching out and analyzing the symbolic forms—words, images, institutions, behaviors—in terms of which, in each place, people actually represent themselves to themselves and to one another." [13] The import of Geertz's procedure is that in order for outsiders to be able to appreciate what is going on in a different culture they must possess considerable background knowledge. Also presupposed is a fundamental familiarity with the codes and symbols of one's own culture, which provides a basis for comparison and contrast.

Geertz's description of a Balinese artistic performance is interesting in what it can tell us about Balinese values and our own:

> Artistic performances start, go on (often for very extended periods of time when one does not attend continually but drifts away and back, chatters for a while, sleeps for a while, watches rapt for a while), and stop; they are as uncentered as a parade, as directionless as a pageant. Ritual often seems, as in the temple celebrations, to consist largely of getting ready and cleaning up. The heart of the ceremony . . . is deliberately muted to the point where it sometimes seems almost an afterthought. . . . It is all welcoming and bidding farewell, foretaste and aftertaste. . . . Even in such a dramatically more heightened ceremony as the Rangda-Barong . . . [one experiences] a mystical, metaphysical, and moral standoff, leaving everything precisely as it was, and the observer—or anyway the foreign observer—with the feeling that something decisive was on the verge of happening but never quite did. [14]

If one considers Western ideas about aesthetic experience and the emphasis they place on the Aristotelian unities—for example, on beginnings, middles, climaxes, and ends—then nothing could seem more alien to Western sensibilities than the character of Balinese artistic performances. Where Western dramatic performances are faulted if they are too long or if they drag, a Balinese performance seems to be largely indifferent to its temporal aspects. Where a Western dramatic production intentionally creates tension and suspense and punctuates the action with points of heightened interest, the Balinese counterpart seems to lack focus and direction. Where in Western drama resolutions of dramatic conflict and tension are characteristic, in Balinese drama the action is deliberately attenuated and muted. There is no forward propulsion to speak of, no gathering of momentum toward an exciting conclusion. Like Balinese life itself, Balinese art and ritual lack movement and climax, or they lack climax because they lack movement. To take Balinese artistic performances at face value then would be to miss their point. A proper understanding would require moving back and forth through Kaufmann's concentric circles—from a performance itself to the various contexts of Balinese culture, and so forth.

To be sure, Geertz says that all of this is not to deny what is apparent even to the uninformed percipient—that aesthetic considerations pervade Balinese life. Great attention is paid to form and style, and enormous importance is attached to pleasing others aesthetically. But he points out the importance of understanding the distinctive roles that aesthetic form and style play in Balinese life. In Bali, art is one of the means by which all aspects of personal life are stylized to the point where anything characteristic of the individual, of the self behind the mask or the person behind the facade presented to the world, is intentionally obliterated. "It is dramatic personae," writes Geertz, "not actors, that in the proper sense really exist. Physically men come and go—mere incidents in a happenstance history of no genuine importance, even to themselves. But the masks they wear, the stage they occupy, the parts they play, and, most important, the spectacle they mount remain and comprise not the facade but the substance of things, not least the self."[15]

It is difficult to imagine a more striking contrast to the Western ideal of selfhood, which places so much importance on the development of personality and self-fulfillment. We need only recall the classical ideal of excellence that stresses the encouragement, achievement, and recognition of outstanding accomplishment. Far from requiring the negation of the self, the classical ideal insists on its intensification through the cultivation of a personal style that prompts one to try to stand out against others. The Western concept of self typically exhorts individuals to participate fully in the contest of life, to experience striving, success, and failure—a primordial struggle for which Jacob wrestling with the angel is a more appropriate image than the dissolution of the self through aesthetic etiquette. This is a radically alternative view of selfhood, or of an absence of such, which provides an opportunity for critical reflection about one's own attitude toward selfhood.

Trilling engaged in precisely such critical reflection when he pondered the adequacy of traditional methods of literary criticism. The question was not one of imitating the outward appearance of a different culture—the road taken, for example, by the youth culture of the sixties, whose mode of dress prompted Saul Bellow to liken the university campus to the back lot of a Hollywood studio, or the path taken by those who encourage blacks to adopt a traditional African look. Rather, for Trilling the problem was a more basic, structural one—the actual possibility of life approximating art. Deeply knowledgeable about his own intellectual and cultural traditions, Trilling points out that such a prospect is actually not as foreign to Western intellectual beliefs as might be thought. Toward the end of his essay on Austen, he observes:

> We of the West are never finally comfortable with the thought of life's susceptibility to being made into aesthetic experience, not even when the idea is dealt with as one of the received speculations of our intellectual culture—sooner or later, for example, we find ourselves becoming uneasy with Schiller's having advanced, on the basis of Kant's aesthetic theory, the idea that life will be the better for transforming itself into art, and we are uneasy again with Huizinga's having advanced the proposition, on the basis of Schiller's views, that life actually does transform itself into art: we feel that both authors deny the earnestness and literalness—the necessity—of which, as we of the West ultimately feel, the essence of life consists.

Nonetheless, in what were perhaps some of his last written words, Trilling urged that "it is open to us to believe that our alternations of view on this matter of life seeking to approximate art are not a mere display of cultural indecisiveness but, rather, that they constitute a dialectic, with all the dignity that inheres in that word." [16]

Had Trilling been a sympathetic reader of John Dewey, he would also have found such an openness in *Art as Experience*. Yet with its dramatic Aristotelian organization of elements even Dewey's notion of aesthetic experience is incompatible with the Balinese concept of self, although there is no question that Dewey would have looked favorably on Bali's integration of aesthetic values into practically all aspects of life.

It should be clear by now what Kaufmann means by the dialectical reading of a classical text and what I mean by a dialectical engagement of the arts of a different culture, either a non-Western culture or a past period in one's own cultural heritage. Trilling, who exemplifies Kaufmann's ideal dialectical reader, was no exegeticist or dogmatist. And he was hardly agnostic in Kaufmann's sense of the term. In his dialecticism—he mentions the dignity that inheres in the word *dialectical*—he continued to remain open to alternative visions of the self. The student of the arts of different cultures should be no less open to alternative visions. Even it if happens that a different culture has little to add to one's concept of selfhood, there is still a gain: an increased awareness of one more of the myriad ways in which individuals live out their lives.

A study of cultural diversity, which is less than dialectical and undertaken primarily for political reasons, holds potential for distortion and self-deception. The discussion has further cautioned against the dangers that arise when one attempts to navigate a different society without a good knowledge of one's own traditions. But this warning also spotlights an anomaly. We are being urged to undertake multicultural studies at a time when a shockingly high level of cultural illiteracy in our own society is being reported. Although we have obviously failed to traverse the concentric circles of our own world, we are being asked to traverse the concentric circles of other cultures. Perhaps then we may trade on Kaufmann's image of concentric circles for thinking about civilizations themselves. The innermost circle for Americans would be Western civilization, whose peculiar voice and influence on American civilization should be studied first. The next circle would then consist of those civilizations that have impinged most significantly on Western and American civilization. All of this would be taken care of before beginning the study of radically different cultures, which would occupy the third circle. This way of thinking is emphasized in the discussion of a cultural literacy curriculum in chapter 6.

Four discussions of multiculturalism highlight current thinking on trends and issues. The first, "Pluralism as a Basis for Educational Policy: Some Second Thoughts" by Mary Ann Raywid, a philosopher of education, anticipated much of what has come to pass. The second discussion, "Multiculturalism: E Pluribus Plures" by Diane Ravitch, a historian of American education, marks a transition in thinking about multiculturalism from a point of view that approves of initiating the young into a richly varied common culture to one that rejects universalism and multiculturalism in favor of cultural particularism and separatism. A third discussion, "The New Musical Correctness and Its Mistakes," by Edward Rothstein, a music critic, questions the concept of cultural equity he finds implicit in numerous proposals for multicultural education, while in "Art, Culture, and Identity," John Wilson, a British philosopher of education, recommends a culture-free education rooted in an ideal of worthwhileness.[17]

The general context of Raywid's remarks is the peculiar psychic pain that affects modern existence, a feeling of rootlessness and not belonging that is intensified by an awareness of powerlessness in the face of large and impersonal social structures. The consequent search for identity and security within a cultural group and the sense of empowerment believed to follow from it, she hypothesizes, account for much of the appeal exerted by what in the mid-seventies was called the "new ethnicity."

Drawing on social theory and conceptualizations of ethnicity, Raywid explains that the "new" in the new ethnicity consists of the extension of earlier ways of establishing identity through religion and nationality to ways that stress racial and gender differences. Theorists of the time claimed that this new ethnicity was characterized by a shared feeling of peoplehood, a key element of which was delight in subtle expressions of the soul and in certain reflections, imaginings, and historical experiences rather than in ideas and words. A common history or ancestry was held to be crucial above anything else. In contrast to melting-pot theories of assimilation, analyses of ethnicity tended to stress difference. What European immigrants really wanted, it was claimed, was not a redefinition of themselves, but the opportunity to pursue their old ways free of the aggravations that plagued them in their native lands. This view conflicts with the belief that the unique circumstances of American life offered immigrants a chance to create a new kind of person, not an Irish American or an Italian American, for example, but an American with a distinct national character. The new ethnicity rejected such a view, insisting instead that people can be held together only by a mystical ethnic bond, a bond that implies taboos on certain sentiments and behaviors. Groups in which such a bond exists cannot properly be considered voluntary associations, for they exact too much conformity and resistance to outsiders. Neither could one simply make a pretense of being a member or go only half way. Increasingly, the trend was toward an insular pluralism, or what Ravitch later would call "cultural particularism."

Raywid acknowledges that cultural pluralism makes significant contributions to American civilization. Not only can it preserve cultural traditions and provide career opportunities for different cultural groups, but it can also foster a sense of self-worth and importance. She questions whether pluralism is the proper remedy for the psychic pain of modern existence. Might there not be some unwanted consequences for both the individual and society? Raywid even wonders whether pluralism could really work, and she is particularly troubled by its emphasis on ascriptive rights rather than on achievement. In 1975, she wrote:

Cultural pluralism apportions functions and statuses within society by ascription in contrast to achievement. Such an arrangement is logically implicit in the promise the group makes its own, reserving all functions to be performed by group members. The selection occurs, then, by virtue of birth. We have associated democracy and the open society with the ending of privilege by birthright—and with the insistence that the individual be able to make his or her own way. . . . Yet the new ethnicity seems not only to be returning to ascribed statuses, but bent on legitimizing and extending them to an unprecedented extent. Its success seems evident in the spread of Affirmative Action programs and quota systems barring status assignment on a strict achievement basis that is sex-blind or race-blind, and instead pursuing justice via what has been called "see-saw discrimination." [18]

Raywid raises the question of the efficacy of cultural pluralism and how socially maladaptive it might prove to be. Is it congruent with the demands of the larger society in which ethnic members must live, work, and raise their children? What will be the individual and social consequences of an insistence that persons with different ethnic identities maintain a closer allegiance to their ancestors than to the realities of contemporary metropolitan life? Is there not even an incipient totalitarianism in a return to ritualistic tribalism, what with its subordination of the individual to the group and its demands for deference, loyalty, and obedience? In short, Raywid worries that anti-individualism and antihumanitarism could be among the unintended and unwanted consequences of the new ethnicity.

But more is at stake than the possible adverse effects of ethnicity on individuals; social cohesion could be sundered. Just as too much uniformity undermines democracy, so does excessive pluralism. In terms that anticipated E. D. Hirsch's concern about the decline of cultural literacy and its effect on social unity, Raywid asserts that "it is obvious that society, community, even limited communication require the sharing of a minimal core of ideas and folkways" (93). Would pluralism's emphasis on difference jeopardize even this bare minimum? Clearly, Raywid is apprehensive that the centrifugal forces inherent in pluralism will erect barriers against group members' participation in the larger society, an apprehension that Ravitch also expresses. Raywid further believes that encouraging the young to achieve self-definition in relation to chosen enemies will likely lead to greater social conflict. The new ethnicity she describes dissuades ethnic members from forming effective relationships beyond their own groups, even though they will ultimately have to live a large part of their lives outside them. Consequently, Raywid questions whether the new ethnicity holds any significant potential for healing alienation and powerlessness. She even suggests that it may be just one more attempt to escape from freedom, for the effort to loosen the hold of the larger society in favor of the ethnic group actually creates a tighter bondage. The niche that surrounds and warms also imprisons and restricts.

Raywid is better at raising questions then prescribing changes, yet she does make some recommendations. She calls for new social forms that are not xenophobic and do not exact all of a member's loyalty or obedience, but rather would secure cohesion through common interests. An individual might participate in several such groups. She also stresses the need for universalism in order to counteract the harmful consequences of cultural separatism and particularism. By "universalism" she implies "the tendency . . . to stress the similarity and brotherhood of peoples, and to promulgate a common core of beliefs and common standards to which all can aspire and against which all should be judged" (97). In particular, she underlines the importance and inevitability of standards, of the necessity to make distinctions among better and poorer performance and to acknowledge hierarchies of value. Only an ill-conceived cultural relativism, she argues, can hold that value distinctions are nonexistent or unnecessary. Many cultures distinguish between high and low, elite and popular, and recognize gradations of excellence. In the best tradition of humanist criticism, then, Raywid recalls readers to the values of social cohesion, universalism, and judgment, her response to the unwanted consequences of ethnic enclavism.

Fifteen years after Raywid's article, in 1990, Diane Ravitch acknowledged the social injustices that have existed in American society and the progress that has been made in eliminating bias and discrimination against certain groups: "Today's history textbooks routinely incorporate the experience of women, blacks, American Indians, and various immigrant groups."[19] Although Ravitch, like Raywid, is clearly committed to the idea of a richly varied common culture, she assigns a more positive and strategic role to the language of cultural pluralism because she wants to oppose it to an extreme form of ethnicity she terms "cultural particularism." She takes the latter to be a form of fundamentalism that has all the faults Raywid ascribed to the new ethnicity but exceeds it in its ethnocentrism.

Ravitch observes that cultural particularlists, in contrast to cultural pluralists, favor an ethnocentric curriculum that aims to improve the academic achievement of minority group children by enhancing their self-esteem. These goals are to be reached by establishing close ties to a group's land of ancestral origin—Africa for African Americans, Central and South America for Hispanic Americans, pre-Columbian America for Native Americans, and so forth. The most highly developed form of this particularism to date, Afrocentrism, emphasizes Africa as the cradle of civilization, with Egyptian civilization as its core. Unblinking in her description of this form of cultural particularism, Ravitch claims that it

> is unabashedly filiopietistic and deterministic. It teaches children that their identity is determined by their "cultural genes." That something in their blood or race memory or their cultural DNA defines who they are and what they may achieve. That the culture in which they live is not their own culture, even though they were born here. That American culture is "Eurocentric," and therefore hostile to anyone whose ancestors are not European. Perhaps the most invidious implication of particularism is that racial and ethnic minorities are not and should not try to be part of American culture; it implies that American culture belongs only to those who are white and European; it implies that those who are neither white nor European are alienated from American culture by virtue of their race or ethnicity; it implies that the only culture they do belong to or can ever belong to is the culture of their ancestors, even if their families have lived in this country for generations. (341)

The import of such views is that schools should not prepare children to live in a racially and culturally diverse society where the young should develop their abilities and talents within a common culture. "Particularists reject any accommodation among groups, any interactions that blur the distinct lines between them. The brand of history that they espouse is one in which everyone is either a descendant of victims or oppressors. By doing so, ancient hatreds are fanned and recreated in each new generation" (341–42). Raywid's worst fears of increased racial conflict and hostility have thus been realized.

But just as Raywid perceives difficulties in the premises of the new

ethnicity, so Ravitch find serious flaws in the arguments of cultural particularists. They ignore huge differences within cultures that result in
part from intermarriage and linkages across groups. This makes a division into five neat groups meaningless (e.g., African Americans, Asian
Americans, European Americans, Latino and Hispanic Americans, and
Native Americans). Particularists further fail to realize the universal
nature of human accomplishment and the fact that people can be inspired by models from all groups, cultures, and societies and not just by
members of their own group. For example, she quotes a talented black
runner as saying that she admires the dancer Mikhail Baryshnikov because he is a magnificent athlete and has such disciplined control over
his body. The runner's appreciation of outstanding accomplishment, in
other words, transcends race, class, and gender.

Like Raywid, Ravitch sees particularism as dysfunctional and maladaptive. She thinks it unlikely that it will either serve the interests of
those for whose benefit it is intended or bode well for social peace and
cohesion. Particularism also raises insuperable curriculum and pedagogical problems; perhaps most serious of all, it contradicts the liberal
tradition of thought and action whose modern form originated in the
period of the Enlightenment. In scorning the achievements and influence of European civilization, cultural particularists abjure the ideals of
fairness and rationality so basic to contemporary democratic societies.
They display a strong tendency to denounce any criticism or questioning of their ideas as inherently racist, as attempts on the part of a white
dominant majority to maintain power and cultural hegemony. Moreover, the penchant for hyperbole has led to some highly questionable
assertions regarding cultural predestination, for example, African civilization as the source of all creativity and the racial superiority of people
of color. In this latter respect, observes Ravitch, Afrocentrists remind
one of the cold war-era Russian officials who claimed surpassing originality and inventiveness for Russians.

Ravitch believes that reason, rational debate, and even scholarship
are not the primary concerns of cultural particularists. Their aggressive
efforts to gain professional advantage and influence are, she thinks, pure
power plays. Yet the war against Eurocentrism cannot go unanswered,
and Ravitch explains why Americans have good reasons to retain close
ties with Europe. Quite simply, many of our cultural roots, our social,
intellectual, moral, political, and religious traditions, are European.
Eighty percent of Americans are of European descent, and English is

the principal language spoken in this country. Collectively, all of this has created a common culture that it has been the purpose of American schools to transmit in order to make the young effective members of society. Castigating all this as mere Eurocentric arrogance actually endangers the tradition of public education and public support for it. Although Ravitch defends the importance of cultural pluralism in our type of society—and there can be no doubt about her conviction in this regard, as is amply testified by her work with the history curriculum of the state of California—she also believes that

> educators must adhere to the principle of "E Pluribus Unum." That is, they must maintain a balance between the demands of the one—the nation of which we are common citizens—and the many—the varied histories of the American people. It is not necessary to denigrate either the one or the many. Pluralism is a positive value, but it is also important that we preserve a sense of an American community—a society and culture to which we all belong. If there is no overall community with an agreed-upon vision of liberty and justice, if all we have is a collection of racial and ethnic cultures, lacking any common bonds, then we have no means to mobilize public opinion on behalf of people who are not members of our particular group. We have, for example, no reason to support public education. (353)

Ravitch centers on Afrocentrism in her discussion of multiculturalism not only because of what she considers to be its fatal flaws but also because of its potential for generating what she calls "multiple-centrisms" and the intensification of divisiveness. She is also emphatic in stressing the need for sound scholarship. Truth, she argues, is a function neither of power and dogmatic theories of racial superiority nor of unbridled relativism. Only a continuing search that leads to the constant revision and correction of knowledge is defensible.

In a follow-up article, Ravitch acknowledges that she should not have spoken of multicultural particularism in the original article, for whereas multiculturalism implies pluralism, particularism rejects it.[20] The confusion arises because particularists tend to voice their beliefs in multicultural forums. Ravitch argues that because of its extreme ethnocentrism and dogmatism, a better term for cultural particularism is *cultural fundamentalism.* Yet she asks that we not be misled by fundamentalist thinking. Knowledgeable people do not confuse culture and race, cultural affinity and cultural identity, and cultural origin and cultural pre-destination. They recognize the multiple interests of a given cultural group, the tension and conflict that often divide them, the syncretistic value of all cultures whose members intermingle among themselves and with others outside the group, and the universal features of cultures.

As for universalism, Ravitch gives a good example of it when she accepts the relevance of the metaphor of a round table, at which representatives of all groups and culture should be seated without discrimination so long as they keep in mind that the table itself is the democratic political tradition:

> It is the galaxy of political ideas and values that includes liberty, equality, and justice. It is the complex of democratic practices that requires us to respect basic human rights, to listen to dissenters instead of jailing them, to have a multi-party system, a free press, free speech, freedom of religion, freedom of assembly, and free trade unions. It is a tradition shaped by the Enlightenment, by James Otis, Thomas Jefferson, Horace Mann, Ralph Waldo Emerson, Abraham Lincoln, Frederick Douglas, Elizabeth Cady Stanton, Susan B. Anthony, Samuel Gopers, John Dewey, Jane Addams, A. Philip Randolph, Franklin Delano Roosevelt, Martin Luther King, Jr., Bayard Rustin, and millions of other people from different cultural backgrounds.[21]

I am not suggesting, nor do Raywid and Ravitch, that reform along the lines of a greater understanding and appreciation of cultural diversity is unimportant. Ravitch notes with satisfaction that new scholarship has already been responsible for correcting mistakes and filling in lacunae in curriculums. What both authors question is whether some of the proposed reforms will be as efficacious as their advocates suppose. They both insist that accurate knowledge and sound scholarship should underpin curriculum recommendations. Ravitch believes that many of the particularists' claims do not meet this test; they are controversial and have not been subjected to adequate criticism and debate.

The need for scholarly knowledge is what animated a criticism of multiculturalists by the music critic Edward Rothstein, who views multiculturalism as "at bottom, folkish Romanticism gone bad. Its calls for equity derive not from recognized unity, but from enforced difference. It takes other cultures seriously only as representations of the merely particular.

Multiculturalism fails to see the Other within us, or us within the Other. As a result, it undoes the very notion of Western culture." He further believes that "multiculturalism is a twisted version of Western teachings, flourishing in the hothouse of a democracy that renders all distinctions suspect and all learning elitist. The multiculturalist is a Western liberal with so large a power of empathy that liberalism itself is dissolved, a rationalist with so transcendental a perspective that reason itself is discarded. The multiculturalist is a universalist without universalism, an artist without a vision of art; a monster child of Western culture; a baleful, unwitting tribute to the tradition he hungers to depose."[22]

These are harsh and sweeping judgments expressed in language and rhetoric that I would not use. Yet it is worth noting some of the reasons Rothstein gives for believing that multiculturists distort the nature of art music, folk music, ethnicity, and the Western tradition itself.

To begin with, Rothstein acknowledges that despite the security of the Western compositional tradition in both Western and non-Western societies, this tradition is suffering from an internal crisis. Not only the magnification of perennial problems during periods of economic recession must be contended with, but also the failure of the public schools to educate a musically literate audience. Furthermore, members of ethnic groups report experiencing discomfort in the traditional venues required by the performance of largely Western music. Put all this together with the political agenda of multiculturalists and the stage is set for an attack on the Western tradition of composition itself. Rothstein cites a national task force report on the touring performing arts and a *Boston Globe* series of stories in 1991 on musical culture in Boston as indicative of the multiculturalist agenda to bring about "musical correctness," that is, a music culture divorced from the cultural tradition of Western civilization because of the latter's purported racism and elitism.

In discussing the national task force report funded by the Rockefeller Foundation, the Pew Charitable Trusts, and the National Endowment for the Arts, Rothstein draws attention to its central concern with community and cultural equity. The fact that equity is to be understood as serving the objectives of community implies that value distinctions and judgments will be minimized when the arts of different ethnic groups and cultures are under consideration. As if recalling Raywid's remarks about ascriptive rights, Rothstein points out the emphasis the performing arts report places on the right of all groups, irrespective of accomplishment, to equal attention and funding for the creation and performance of music. Accordingly, major social changes are demanded that must be responsive to the grievances of oppressed groups. The call is essentially for ethnic enclavism, with the Western cultural tradition constituting but one enclave among others; having no superior value, it can make no special claims.

The upshot of such a point of view is by now familiar: the politicization of music. Music should no longer be valued principally as a unique art form that by reinterpreting traditional works or by presenting new ones constantly tries to extend itself through the creation of new musical values. Nor should music be encountered and appreciated for its capacity to afford an enriching aesthetic experience. What counts is the ethnic origin and character of a given piece of music. The effect of a commitment to cultural equity is "to redefine the function of the presenter: the urgency is not to reveal something about music itself, not to mount exhibitions and performances on behalf of an artistic vision, not to encourage people to hear things they've never heard before and to engage in acts of musical imagination. The objective is, first and foremost, to achieve 'equity' by serving individual 'communities' without distinction. . . . In the view of the 'multiculturalists,' music is fundamentally 'folk' in character. It functions as a reinforcement of group identity" (30). But all of this, argues Rothstein, is based on several misunderstandings.

First, the war against Eurocentrism in music fails to appreciate the extent to which American musical culture has long been open to the musical values of different cultures, values that have, in turn, enriched American musical culture. Never has this been truer than today. The multicultural crusade against the Eurocentrism of the American musical tradition is thus something of an anomaly, and Rothstein provides several examples of cultural assimilation. But these realities cannot affect the overriding multiculturalist aim of cutting the Western musical tradition down to size. When multiculturalists claim that there can be no cultural hierarchies and no hierarchies of musical value, they are denying critics in American musical culture the right to make distinctions when, in fact, such distinctions are being made in numerous non-Western musical traditions. To support his remarks about music performing different functions in different societies, Rothstein refers to three volumes in the Cambridge Studies in Ethnomusicology series and to the writings of the distinguished musicologist Bruno Nettl.

Regarding the variable functions of music, Rothstein states that the chants of the Amazonian Suya Indians are representative of the character of much folk music, the kind multiculturalists tend to regard as exemplary. Folk art is strongly related to a tradition of performance and ritual and is communal and tribal in character, which is to say it is inseparable from daily life. Both instruments and music tend to reflect premodern social activities. Yet Rothstein points out that not all non-Western music has a folk character or tribal function. Pakistani Sufi music is largely devotional music and intended to induce an ecstatic state of mind and involvement with the words being sung. A feeling of religious transport is an appropriate response. Such music is neither strictly ceremonial, ritualistic, nor intended for analytical listening and contemplation. It is a far cry, moreover, from the chants of Amazonian boatmen as they ply their crafts through the water. Still different in character and function is the high art of Cantonese opera and some other Chinese music that recalls the theater of the Renaissance and the courtly music of seventeenth-century Europe. Such music comes closest to the high art of Western societies. All these categories of music—folk, religious, courtly, aesthetic—interpenetrate and change their interrelationships over time. Categories like these are important, Rothstein thinks, because they "allow us to understand not just what a music succeeds at creating, but what it is attempting to create; they combine social function and stylistic description" (31).

Given popular assumptions about the character of non-Western music, Rothstein uses Bruno Nettl's work to dispel some misconceptions. Nettl points out that whether or not a culture has a high culture, there does exist some kind of hierarchy in the musical system of most cultures, "a continuum from some kind of elite to popular." [23] Nettl also makes clear that wherever civilizations have produced a high musical culture they have been able to do so because of a distinctly self-conscious attitude about music, a formal institutionalization of its teaching, performance, and appreciation, and a long performing tradition with a varied repertoire. In the advanced civilizations of Asia—for example, in India, Iran, and Japan—elite music is objectively studied and easily separated from custom and ordinary life. American Indians and Australian aborigines also have traditions of teaching music, but they are not separate from social functions. The point here is that many societies exhibit some kind of cultural hierarchy, some kind of continuum from elite to popular. The placement of a particular musical form is a matter of the music's complexity and sophistication, subtlety of expression, and intricacy of meaning. Value differentiations are universal and derive in large from basic aesthetic considerations. These distinctions are present whether or not we choose to take notice of them.

Multiculturalists purposely suppress such distinctions in order to concentrate on a work's provenance. But in doing so Rothstein remarks that multiculturalists misunderstand and distort the very cultures they are intent on holding up as significant counterexamples to the West. So intense is their animus against the West that nothing else seems to matter, not even the facts. Among these facts is one mentioned earlier, that the United States is unique in its receptiveness to the music of other civilizations and has been so as part of an endeavor to understand better the nature of music itself, to expand and enrich it. As Rothstein writes, "The non-Western has been as much a part of the phenomenon of music for many Western composers and writers as native works" (33). The picture that emerges from Rothstein's discussion is hardly one of a dominating and oppressive culture impervious to any influences except those emanating from Europe. To balance the equation, many cultures have openly welcomed the influence of Western musical traditions, and composers around the world have acknowledged the efforts of Western composers to advance the art of music.

Rothstein claims that multiculturists do not understand art music, folk music and ethnicity, or Western civilization. They fail to give credit not only to Western musical culture for its openness but also to Western composers and musical analysts for their endeavors to achieve universal validity and autonomy for music. Such a quest can be carried forward only under conditions of freedom for musical composition and criticism, conditions that stand in marked contrast to the constraints inherent in folk music traditions. Freedom must prevail not only for composers, theorists, and critics of music, but also for listeners of music, for a democratic society has a commitment to make music available to all wanting to experience its peculiar qualities.

A choice of terms can prejudice attitudes. Critics of Western cultural values see such values as reflections of dominant and oppressive institutions. But it is just as appropriate and certainly more useful to emphasize the West's ideals of toleration, freedom of expression, and individual empowerment. Institutions established to provide opportunities for human development and free, personal expression may not always succeed as intended, but that does not justify dismantling them or denying their obvious accomplishments. Some multiculturalists seem bent on repudiating not only most of what Western societies have accomplished but also the ideals and commitments that made such attainments possible. Rothstein therefore laments the move from a progressive ethnomusicology and anthropology to a countercultural romanticism and multicultural fundamentalism, that is, a folkish romanticism gone wrong. The multiculturalist's perversion, he says, is the willful misrepresentation of the liberal tradition and the energies of modernity that, contrary to the multicultural ethos, have helped to create an authentically diverse and ambitiously transcendent culture. It is into this open Western musical tradition that the young should be initiated first. Dialectical encounters with culture, to recall Kaufmann's terminology, should begin at home.

A summary of the points made by Raywid, Ravitch, and Rothstein is in order. Raywid realizes the significant impact that educational policies promoting cultural diversity can have on American schooling. She understands that the new ethnicity constitutes a response to alienation and powerlessness but doubts that these conditions can be alleviated primarily through the cultivation of ethnicity. She understands that the emphasis on ancestral origins and ethnic differences might well generate hostility toward others and that the elevation of ascriptive rights over individual merit could prove dysfunctional and maladaptive. Her concern over possible unwanted consequences of cultural pluralism has been vindicated, for they have all come to pass with a vengeance she could not have imagined. Raywid foresaw, for example, the current downgrading of achievement in favor of a principle of equity. Most important, she perceived the seeds of totalitarian thinking in an ethnic enclavism that values group loyalty and solidarity more highly than individual freedom and achievement. Raywid further anticipated E. D. Hirsch and his alarm over a slippage in the general background knowledge shared by Americans so serious as to threaten the ideal of a common culture.

Ravitch's analysis is valuable because it indicates how much of what Raywid feared has actually happened. Ravitch also provides a terminology for further discussion and debate; for example, she suggests *cultural particularism* as a term for the phenomenon Raywid had called "insular pluralism" and identifies particularism as a form of fundamentalist thinking that has all the faults, and then some, of the new ethnicity. Rothstein, finally, traces the evolution of politically correct thinking into music. He characterizes the multiculturalists' views of music as a folkish romanticism, the roots of which can be found in the countercultural 1960s. The multiculturalists' misconceptions about ethnicity and ethnic art, their refusal to distinguish better from poorer and elite from popular art, and their misrepresentation of Western civilization are all consequences, he believes, of a power movement that sweeps facts, rationality, and common sense aside in the single-minded pursuit of political aims.

Raywid's, Ravitch's, and Rothstein's discussions of multiculturalism stayed close to home, so to speak. A more distanced and generalized perspective questions one of the multiculturalist's most basic and unexamined assumptions.

In a discussion of the concepts of art, culture, and identity, John Wilson, a British philosopher, critically examines the belief, emphatically subscribed to by multiculturalists, that the best way to achieve a secure sense of self is through a strong identification with one's cultural origins. In opposition to the idea of cultural equity favored by many multiculturalists, Wilson recommends a culture-free education grounded in what is valuable and worthwhile.

Wilson first defines his key terms. By "art" he understands anything that can be viewed aesthetically, that is, with a keen interest in an object's elegance, charm, beauty, and so forth. The things that reward such an interest most gratifyingly are, of course, works of art, and to experience works of art aesthetically is not to be preoccupied with their material dimensions or with their cognitive, moral, and political values. Wilson thinks aesthetic experience is important because it seems to be a basic form of human life. "If," he observes, "we take 'the aesthetic viewpoint' in a sufficiently wide and sufficiently pedestrian sense, then that viewpoint is something we are landed with. All people . . . order their lives and surroundings, sometimes, for nonutilitarian purposes and purposes that are not directly connected with enterprises like religion or politics." [24] As for "culture," Wilson accepts what has become its standard meaning, the rules, practices, forms of life, styles, and values — including aesthetic activities and values — that characterize human social groups. The notion of "identity," however, suggests something more personal and individual, a feeling of being psychologically secure that may derive from a network of cultural experiences to which persons have become accustomed. Yet Wilson asks whether a sense of psychological security ought to be grounded solely in one's own culture and whether there may not be danger in tying one's identity so closely to cultural features that are inherently fragile and changeable.

Wilson makes three points. Similar to Raywid, he thinks that grounding identity primarily in one's cultural origins may be less important than grounding it in other values. Religious beliefs, family values, economic security, political activity, and physical or artistic prowess, for example, may count for more than ancestry. Emphasis on such outward aspects as a person's color or on indicators of social class would also be misplaced. The personal, psychological elements in an individual's make-up are likely to be more significant, and there is little reason for believing that elevated social status is a guarantor of contentment. It is not, Wilson acknowledges, that cultural and social factors are negligible; they may loom large at a certain time in a person's life. Perhaps everyone lives through a developmental stage that pays great attention to cultural and social considerations. But given their susceptibility to rapid change, such features may not in the long run be reliable ingredients of a stable identity.

Wilson's point may be illustrated by a reference to the great sensitivity of some ethnic groups to matters of terminology (what they wish to be called) and outward appearance, for example, the recommendation that black Americans should adopt African names and dress. Many blacks, however, ignore such prescriptions and suggest by this decision that such external signs of identity are less important than other things. What is more, uncritical admirers of a certain culture preoccupied with imitating its surface features may blind themselves to its faults. In this respect Wilson agrees with Eaton's assertion (in chapter 4) that some cultures, or some aspects of them, do not deserve admiration. Wilson criticizes the attitude that treasures whatever a person calls "mine"— these are my ancestors, my social practices, and so forth—because it provides no assurance that the things thus prized are true, worthwhile, or valuable. What is true, worthwhile, and valuable transcends race, class, and gender.

An education that seeks to transcend the values bound up with particular cultures would in a sense be culture-free. Although it would not deny the importance of considerations of culture, race, and gender, it would remind individuals that building a significant sense of self means coming to realize the limitations and shortcomings of such categories. On the other hand, a commitment to transcendental values like the good, the true, and the beautiful does not confine the self, but liberates it for the pursuit of really worthwhile things.

Any educator, indeed any serious person, ought on reflection to realize that identity or security ought *not* to be sought in one's culture, that all of us have to be weaned and helped away from our cultures toward what is truly valuable and in a transcendental culture-free way, and that it is at best patronizing and trivial, at worst crippling and cruel, to encourage particular cultures to adore themselves in mirrors. Instead of feeling narcisstic (or guilty) about one's culture, one should have something better to do. Art . . . is one of these better things. (96)

Wilson clearly recognizes the interdependence of his three concepts. Culture is the all-embracing context within which one strives to achieve identity, a context that includes activities that we know as art and that may for some people be important determinants of self. Wilson perhaps misleads when he stresses elegance, charm, and beauty as central features of works of art, unless, that is, beauty is assumed to include the artistic expression of some of the more unpleasant and tragic aspects of life as well. But his concern in this instance is not with precise definition or extensive qualification; it is with marking the distinctive character that the aesthetic lends to some experiences. For more detailed accounts of the aesthetic and related concepts, the standard literature of aesthetics may be consulted.[25]

Although Wilson grants that a person's ancestral origin can play an important part in shaping identity, it may often not be the most important determinant. He would endorse Raywid's suggestion that identity not be sought exclusively within one's primary cultural group, but in new social groupings that encourage members to share things in common, things and activities that unite rather than divide. He agrees with Raywid's concern about some of the possibly unwanted consequences of cultural pluralism and the new ethnicity, with Ravitch's apprehension about the potential divisiveness of cultural particularism, and with Rothstein's critique of multiculturalism's commitment to cultural equity.

The question of multiculturalism has individual, social, and political dimensions. The challenge to a theory of education is how to help individuals achieve a sense of self and psychological security in a society that values both individual freedom and social cohesion, a society in which persons in the pursuit of one worthwhile goal do not neglect or deprecate other valuable objectives. The question for a general education curriculum that includes arts education is how to determine the weight that should be given to the arts of different cultures and groups in a society heavily influenced by West European traditions. Wilson's notion of a "culture-free education" does not imply a cultural shopping mall. He merely means that the schools should refrain from enforcing a narrow ethnocentrism.

Two more critical contributions to the literature, which I can only mention here, are by Arthur Schlesinger, Jr., and Midge Decter. Schlesinger's text, *The Disuniting of America*, is essentially a response to Ravitch's plea that sound scholarship should inform decisions about curriculum change, whereas Decter's "E Pluribus Nihil: Multiculturalism and Black Children" ponders some of the potentially tragic consequences for minority children caught in the crossfire of the multicultural political wars.[26]

CHAPTER SIX

The Arts, General Knowledge, and Curriculum

W HAT MIGHT a curriculum for arts education be like that features the development of cultural literacy in the thin and thick senses of the term? How can such a curriculum do justice to both Hirsch's concern to convey a national literate vocabulary and the study in depth that is required for an adequate understanding and enjoyment of works of art? Moreover, how do Hirsch's two curriculums—the extensive curriculum and the intensive curriculum—overlap and reinforce each other? What in particular does Hirsch's idea of cultural literacy contribute to current theories of art education? Where does contextualism fit in?

In a number of places, I have recommended an arts education curriculum that features rationales for general education, redefinitions of the traditional humanities, theories of aesthetic experience, cognitive learning theory, and discipline-based conceptions of teaching art. Depending on the context, I have called such a curriculum an "art world curriculum," a "percipience curriculum," and a "humanities-based curriculum." I would have no reservations about calling it a cultural literacy curriculum as well except for some writers' objections to using the term *literacy* in connection with understanding nonverbal forms of expression. Accordingly, I will refer to a cultural percipience curriculum, where the term *percipience* implies a knowing perception in general and is not restricted to verbal literacy.

Percipience in matters of art and culture is the general goal of arts education. Culturally percipient individuals are art world sojourners who experience works of art with tact and sensitivity and derive from them the worthwhile benefits that works of art at their best are capable of providing. The cultivation of a disposition to appreciate excellence in art is the essence of arts education. Cultural percipience, the knack of knowing one's way around works of art and their various contexts, can be developed by having the young pass through a humanities-based curriculum that consists of five phases of aesthetic learning: exposure plus familiarization and perceptual training in the early years, and historical, appreciative, and critical studies in the later years. With regard to Hirsch, a cultural percipience curriculum may also be understood as a combination of extensive and intensive learning.

A cultural percipience curriculum is grounded in a philosophy of general education that is justified on the basis of its intellectual, moral, and aesthetic commitments. Intellectually, general education provides interpretive frameworks that all citizens need in order to understand and communicate with each other and act in behalf of the common good. Morally, general education is devoted to ensuring the values of a just and compassionate democratic society. And aesthetically, general education is committed to helping persons realize value from the arts and the humanities.

Anyone reading these lines who is familiar with the literature of the philosophy of education will realize that my thinking about general education has been strongly influenced by an esteemed colleague of many years, Harry S. Broudy, one of this country's most distinguished humanists and philosophers of education. Broudy's philosophy of general education is a response to the challenges that a modern democratic mass society faces, a society characterized by technological and information overload, specialism, and the pitfalls of planning. These conditions threaten to lead to the abandonment of moral and aesthetic attitudes in favor of economic and technical solutions to problems. Broudy believes that society can be "remoralized" only by repudiating extreme reductionism in the realm of values.[1]

Of particular significance is Broudy's analysis of the uses of schooling and his belief that the interpretive and associative uses of learning have been slighted in favor of replicative and applicative uses. Replication of learning trains the ability to memorize and reinstate numerous items exactly as they were learned in school. Although replication is obviously necessary for the accomplishment of many tasks, it is helpful only when care is taken to select those items worth replicating. Applicative uses of learning develop skills and knowledge that will later be applied in specific situations, but application becomes irrelevant when taught in ways that are more appropriate for specialists than for generalists. The interpretive and associative uses of learning, on the other hand, are the ones that enable ordinary citizens to make sense of most of the situations they encounter.

Broudy's point is that interpretation presupposes contexts and specific knowledge of the kind that cannot always be recalled and replicated as learned or as applied in the manner of the problem-solving specialist. The reason is that sense-making is a function of a residue of both formal and informal learning and experience that has become enfolded in what Broudy calls the "allusionary base" of the mind. As he puts it in "Cultural Literacy and General Education," the act of interpretation "often requires defining or explaining a situation or a term, and the means for doing so are the residues of a complex of learnings acquired in school. Sometimes we can identify the items as learned in school. Often, however, we attribute our ability to interpret situations to a complex of experiences that we may or may not be able to specify precisely, but which had been imbedded in this or that course." Of the associative uses of learning, Broudy says that they are even less directly connected with specific content. Material used associatively "includes more than school experience, although much of what is studied in formal schooling suggests connections and ideas that were not specifically studied."[2]

Broudy finds philosophical and psychological support for the importance of interpretive and associative uses of schooling in Michael Polanyi's theory of tacit knowing, a central feature of which is Polanyi's seemingly paradoxical statement that we know more than we can tell. It follows that learners may also know more than some test results reveal. To illustrate what Polanyi means, Broudy reacted (in a manner recalling Gombrich's thoughts on the sources of his knowledge of the Judgment of Paris) to a random sample of entries in the *Dictionary of Cultural Literacy* prepared by Hirsch and his colleagues.

Broudy admits that the extent of his familiarity with the items exceeded his ability to account for his familiarity. He explains that although he was unable to replicate the meanings of the items as he had once learned them, he was responding with background experiences that he could not at that moment bring into consciousness "but which had been deposited in what may be called the allusionary base or store" (12). In other words,

> The associative and interpretive uses of schooling provide many of the resources *with* which we think, perceive, and appreciate, but to which at any given moment we are not paying explicit attention. Thus, much of the schooling acquired by direct study tends to fold back into the allusionary base from which relevant items are summoned—not always consciously or deliberately—as the occasion demands. This store of associative material plays a strategic role in any definition of cultural literacy, except perhaps that which identifies the concept with the recollection of names, dates, events, and so forth. (13)

It is clear that Broudy finds Hirsch's concept of cultural literacy too limited and supportive of uses of schooling that are less important than those Broudy would emphasize. But for the most part Broudy concentrates on what Hirsch calls the intensive curriculum of the secondary years, about which Hirsch remains largely silent, his primary interest being in the extensive curriculum of the early years. Broudy is further concerned to refute the arguments of deconstructionists who deny the importance traditionally assigned to the humanities as sources of intellectual, moral, and aesthetic values. Broudy's response stresses the humanities' quest for truth and human significance and the anchoring of warranted value commitments in their credibility.

Although Broudy would want some distinctions made, he would also agree with Gombrich that the great works of the cultural heritage are a wellspring of general knowledge, even when acquaintance with them is relatively superficial. The study of the cultural heritage would, however, be much more empowering if studied for systematic value exploration in some depth, yet still at a nonspecialist level and with the realization that many items will not be recalled as learned originally. Broudy thinks that

> The disciplines studied explicitly in school become resources used tacitly in life; their details are forgotten, leaving frames or lenses or stencils of interpretation, both of fact and value. Perspective and context are the functional residues of general education. We understand *with* them, even though we are not attending to them. I believe that a convincing case can be made for the func-

tionality of formal course work in the associative and interpretive uses of knowledge, even though the content of the formal courses cannot be recalled on cue.[3]

The study of the arts and humanities (or the arts as humanities) makes a threefold contribution to cultural percipience: They are sources of aesthetic enjoyment and humanistic insight, models of excellence deserving of emulation, and input to the mind's allusionary base and imagic store. The specialized study of the arts and humanities in higher education, however, seldom permits the appreciation of their full plenitude of values. Clifton Olds's interpretation of the *St. Luke* painting discussed in chapter 4 can serve as an example of the academic scholar's interest. He makes no mention of the work's excellence or capacity to provide aesthetic enjoyment. Broudy would ensure they were not neglected.

Broudy concludes his remarks in "Cultural Literacy and Arts Education" with a reference to *Democracy and Excellence in American Secondary Education* (1964), which he coauthored with two colleagues, as having been an attempt to cultivate cultural literacy—although not in Hirsch's sense. *Democracy and Excellence* is about secondary education, the locus of what Hirsch calls the intensive curriculum.

There are still other parallels between Hirsch's and Broudy's thinking. In addition to the significance they ascribe to contextual understanding, Hirsch in terms of schema theory and Broudy in terms of Polanyi's theory of tacit knowing, both reject excessive pluralism in favor of the core of common values that Gunnar Myrdal articulated, that Hirsch referred to as America's civil religion, and that Broudy, following Myrdal, called the American Creed. Both writers are liberals who want greater social justice and compassion for underprivileged groups. Both are educational reformers rather than revolutionists. Finally, Hirsch's interest in schema theory and contextual understanding is comparable to Broudy's interest in tacit knowledge. These similarities are not meant to justify each writer in terms of the other but rather to indicate why someone familiar with the work of Broudy might be sympathetic to Hirsch.

In his later writings, Broudy has paid more attention to the early years of schooling, particularly to helping teachers gain an understanding of some of the basic aspects and functions of works of art. But his argument for general education has not changed. In this connection, his emphasis on associative and interpretive uses of learning in general education may have kept Broudy from appreciating sufficiently Hirsch's insistence on the accumulation of basic factual knowledge. Although it is true that, as Broudy states, adults no longer have command of details of knowledge that allowed them to pass tests in school, they needed to have acquired these items at some time in order to possess them tacitly and use them associatively and interpretively. Unless children are provided facts, we cannot hope to reverse a situation in which, as Gombrich says, the past is becoming so dim as to be fading altogether from memory.

The sketch of a curriculum for cultural literacy presented in this chapter—that is, percipience in matters of art and culture—reflects numerous influences on my thinking. Like Walter Clark, whose views on literature were discussed in chapter 4, I am a product of a program of liberal studies in the early fifties that disposed me to an appreciation of the values of a general education, an education comprised of core subjects and some electives, which in my case was coursework in art history. Graduate studies at a teachers' college during the late fifties impressed on me three thousand years of educational wisdom and the problems of schooling in a democratic society. Given some curiosity and a philosophical and speculative bent, I was drawn toward the justification question in arts education. Of what worth is art, and why should people spend their time finding out about it? My undergraduate coursework in art history had convinced me that history is an indispensable source of knowledge that deepens the enjoyment of art (coursework in Northern and Italian Renaissance art is indelibly imprinted on my imagination), and the numerous puzzles involved in defining, interpreting, and evaluating works of art drew me to the philosophy of art, or, the same thing, philosophical aesthetics. Analyses of art's functions by aestheticians also proved helpful in framing a philosophy of arts education, which because of my interest in art in general that I increasingly came to call aesthetic education.

All of the foregoing was background to my starting the interdisciplinary *Journal of Aesthetic Education* in 1966. The general mission of the journal is to publish scholarly articles about art and arts education and related areas. Among other things, this has meant efforts to indicate the relevance of several key disciplines to the teaching of art. With the increasing popularity of art in society, which gave rise to the National Endowment for the Arts and a number of other public and private agencies that became involved in arts education, I also became interested in the problems of defining cultural and educational relations and have done some policy analysis and criticism.

All along, I have retained an interest in the humanities, especially art history; but as an editor I have not been as successful in inducing art historians to write about arts education as I have been in encouraging philosophers of art and the humanities to do so. As a coordinator of a community college humanities project that involved faculty from around the country, I had been somewhat successful in suggesting ways that the arts and humanities could be integrated. In addition to the reception of my ideas in the field of art education, my interests received recognition by the Getty Center for Education in the Arts, with its notions of discipline-based art education. The principal assumption of discipline-based art education (DBAE) is that art is best taught when it is grounded in the ideas and procedures of four interrelated disciplines: artistic creation, art history, art criticism, and aesthetics. I concluded that this approach in effect defines art education in terms of humanities education, and I began to talk about teaching art as a humanity.[4]

A happy circumstance was that before the Getty Center's involvement in art education I had read Albert William Levi's *The Humanities Today*, which contains a persuasive redefinition of the humanities for the modern world.[5] Levi, a distinguished humanist and philosopher of culture, redefined the humanities as the liberal arts of communication, continuity, and criticism, the substance of which he associates with the disciplines of languages and literature, history, and philosophy in its ordinary sense of critical reflection. He thus fuses the procedural with the substantive aspects of the humanities and anticipates by fifteen years Hirsch's effort in this respect.

Obvious parallels, although no precise matches, between Levi's three arts and the Getty's four disciplines suggested themselves, and Levi and I coauthored a volume that presented a rationale for discipline-based art education that featured his redefinition of the humanities.[6] This redefinition is central to the cultural percipience curriculum presented in this chapter. It synthesizes several strands of my thinking: an abiding interest in art history, art criticism (I have long held that the appropriate model for the teacher of art is not the artist but the educative critic), aesthetics, and, of course, artistic creation.

I am conscious of the fact that what follows might be seen as an effort to bring together writers whose ideas do not seem to combine comfortably. My defense is that a unitary, consistent, elegant theory of the kind we tend to find in the sciences seldom does justice to the practical activities of schooling, which require the resources of several disciplines. I hope what follows reflects a principled and informed eclecticism.

My thinking about a humanities-based curriculum for arts education was first set out in an article published in 1968 in the *Teachers College Record*.[7] Since then one of my principal concerns has been to draw attention to the capacity of artworks to provide aesthetic experiences of appreciable magnitude. The writings of Harry S. Broudy, Monroe C. Beardsley, Harold Osborne, E. F. Kaelin, and Marcia M. Eaton are all helpful for this purpose. These writers all believe that aesthetic experience constitutes an important kind of value realization and that works of art are preeminently capable of inviting and sustaining aesthetic interest. None of the ideas of these writers, moreover—nor my own, for that matter—assert that the aesthetic function is the only one artworks perform or that it was their predominant function in times past. It is simply that, as Beardsley once put it, the capacity to provide a certain kind of psychological experience commonly referred to as aesthetic experience is a preeminent or characteristic function of artworks. Like these writers, I also took for granted the importance of contextual knowledge of art (a rich appreciative mass, allusionary base, tacit knowledge, and memory) and felt no need for extended comment about it.

The continuing predominance of process-centered theories of arts education and new revelations of cultural amnesia have, however, made it imperative to place more explicit stress than before on the necessity for contextual knowledge. Calling on my own experience and some relevant contextualist theories of art (as I discussed in chapter 4, not all contextualist theories are helpful), and with the realization that I might have overstated the case for aesthetic experience, I began to think of arts education more in terms of humanities education than of aesthetic education, although what is best in the idea of aesthetic education was carried along. First in *Excellence in Art Education*, then in *The Sense of Art*, and most recently in *Art Education: A Critical Necessity* and a National Society for the Study of Education yearbook *The Arts, Education, and Aesthetic Knowing*, I have been recommending the teaching of art as a humanity.[8] What this volume adds to a humanities-based idea of arts education is Hirsch's notion of cultural literacy and its extensive curriculum and the observations and insights of the contributors to *Cultural Literacy and Arts Education.*

In *The Humanities Today*, Levi distinguishes two traditional definitions of the humanities, one associated with the Middle Ages and the other with the Renaissance.

> From the first century before Christ (when Varro was writing his lost treatises on the liberal arts) to Martianus Capella in the fourth century A.D. the tradition of "the seven liberal arts" was being slowly established, finally to be given definitive status by Cassiodorus and Isidore of Seville in the two centuries following. That the trivial arts of grammar, rhetoric, and dialectic were skills to be taught was self-evident, and even the quadrivium—arithmetic, geometry, astronomy, and music (the first three of which we should today term *sciences*)—were presented as practical arts. Arithmetic, usually discussed in connection with the abacus was "the art of calculating." Geometry, often indistinguishable from geography, was practically equated with surveying and remained close to its etymology as "earth-measurement." Even astronomy was intimately related to the practical problems of the fixing of the calendar and the computation of the date of Easter. These conceptions lasted well into the fourteenth century.
>
> The radical revision of Renaissance education shifts the center of focus in such a way that arts are imperceptibly transformed into subject matters. Logic, not originally burdened with metaphysical problems, became so increasingly in the course of the late Middle Ages. The Renaissance and Enlightenment distinction between natural, metaphysical, and moral philosophy augmented subject-matter concern. The emergent nationalisms gave to history a new thematic importance, and the rise of the vernacular languages and their literary products turned the philological emphasis of grammar further in the direction of the investigation and study of literary content. Not the seven liberal arts, but the languages and literatures, history, and philosophy have become increasingly the claimants for humanistic attention.[9]

Not wishing to abandon either tradition, Levi identifies the humanities with the liberal arts. But he does so in a way that redefines them as the arts of communication, continuity, and criticism, which, once more, coincide with the subjects of languages and literature, history, and philosophy. This enables him to preserve the basic distinction between the sciences and the arts and to divide each of these into the natural and social sciences and the liberal and the fine arts. When Levi refers to the fine arts he has in mind completed objects that assume a place in history. As "artistic utterances" or "artistic statements" the arts become part of the humanities and can be studied for their distinctive values. This is made clear in *Art Education: A Critical Necessity* and emphasized in the following: "When we perceive the arts as "humanities" it is crucial that we interpret them as a demand that we pause, and in their light, reexamine our own realities, values, and dedications, for the arts not only present life concretely, stimulate the imagination, and integrate the different cultural elements of a society or of an epoch, they also present models for our imitation or rejection, visions and aspirations which mutely solicit our critical response." [10]

Levi realizes that the distinction between the humanities and the sciences, especially between the sciences and the social sciences, cannot be precise. Consequently, he writes of certain tendencies of mind. Although practically anything can be studied from a scientific or humanistic point of view, the humanities pursue values with an earnestness that cannot be found in the sciences, and, ultimately, this is the basis of Levi's distinction between the humanistic complex and the scientific chain of meaning. [11]

With some qualification it is possible to subsume the study of the fine arts under languages and literature, history, and philosophy, or under the arts of communication, continuity, and criticism. As an artistic statement of some significance that has a history and usually requires interpretive and evaluative criticism, a work of art is at once a form of communication, a historical object, and an object for interpretation and judgment. But because of the role that creative activities play in building a sense of art in the young (and, in the terms of this study, also because of Hirsch's concern to improve people's communicative powers), the arts of creation can be added to the arts of communication, continuity, and criticism. The purpose then of a humanities-based curriculum for the teaching of the arts may be said to be the development of cultural percipience (and all that it implies) by bringing to bear in appropriate ways on aesthetic learning the arts of creation, communication, continuity, and criticism—the four *c*s of aesthetic understanding—whose coordinate disciplines are artistic making, art history, art criticism, and aesthetics. A simpler, more direct way of stating the purpose of arts education would be to say that we study the rudiments of art for the sake of satisfying a basic human need—but that is just a beginning.

Why should one opt for a more complex statement of aims? For one thing, a comprehensive interpretation of arts education takes into account a variety of resources needed for building a sense of art. Second, it constitutes a response to the requirements of both tradition and contemporary society, for example, the problems of cultural amnesia, the loss of the historical sense and context for response, the escape from judgment, and so forth. A cultural percipience curriculum is a reaction to the demands of both society and individuals; it has public and private value. Arts education contributes to the realization of the objectives of the humanities, whereas the humanities contribute to the realization of a fuller and more complete life.

This discussion assumes the instrumental value of art and arts education. Art is not studied for its own sake; rather, it serves basic human and social needs. Arts education serves not only its own peculiar objectives but also the objectives of the humanities and of schooling in general, which, in turn, serve the larger public goal of conveying the cultural heritage and the maximizing of individual potentialities. This does not mean that aesthetic instruction always has its eye on future outcomes. The study of art can be immediately satisfying at the same time that it serves and strengthens other values. As Levi puts the matter,

> In the case of the arts of communication this has meant the presentation of languages as forms of life enlarging a limited imagination and producing that mutual sympathy Kant took to be the defining property of social man. In the case of the arts of continuity, comprehending both history proper and the use of the classics of literature and philosophy, presented as elements in a continuous human tradition, this has meant the presentation of a common past in the service of social cohesiveness and enlarged social sensitivity. And finally, in the case of the arts of criticism, this has meant the enlargement of the faculty of criticism, philosophically conceived as intelligent inquiry into the nature and maximization of values. A humane imagination, the forging of a universal social

bond based upon sympathy, and the inculcation of a technique for the realization of values then become the ultimate goals of the liberal arts. (85)

To this we need only add the arts of creation, one of the major modes of human expression that reflects on and interprets reality.

A humanities-based curriculum of arts education devoted to cultivating cultural percipience consists of five phases of aesthetic learning: exposure and familiarization, perceptual training, historical awareness, exemplar appreciation, and critical analysis (Figure 1). Phases one and two encompass that part of the curriculum Hirsch calls the extensive curriculum, although it takes up more than the 50 percent of time he allots to conveying extensive information. Phases three through six constitute what Hirsch calls the intensive curriculum and reflect my interpretation. The terms listed under the various arts—for example, time, tradition, and style under the arts of continuity (art history)—suggest centers of interest, although there may be others. The bottom section of the figure reinforces the importance given to the cumulative nature of aesthetic learning.

Although some information about the humanities will be presented in the early phases that feed into later ones, I realize that it may be stretching the meaning of the term *humanities* to apply it to the beginning years. Perhaps we can distinguish between preparatory phases of learning and let humanities study proper start with phase three, with the development of historical awareness. Also, the introduction to the humanities and the art world in the early years occurs in an informal manner that is not to be confused with the disciplined study of the later stages. I do not assume that the five phases of aesthetic learning can be sharply demarcated or that they are strictly correlated with age. Some youngsters upon entering school will be ahead of others and will progress faster. On the whole, however, I think the divisions of the phases are consistent with what we know about human growth and cognitive development.

One of the many things that go without saying—but that nonetheless need re-saying from time to time—is that the development of cultural percipience is a lengthy process that can fill a whole lifetime. It takes time to achieve even a generalist's understanding of the arts and their vari-

General Goal: Cultivating Cultural Percipience in Matters of Art
by Teaching the Concepts and Skills of Art Conceived as a Humanity

Arts of Creation (artistic creation)	Arts of Communication (art as language)	Arts of Continuity (art as history)	Arts of Criticism (aesthetics)
Materials	Artistic statement	Time	Conceptualizing
Techniques	Expression	Tradition	Critical analysis
Artistic decision making	Interpretation	Style	Problem solving
Familiarization, Exposure, and Perceptual Training (Phases 1 and 2, K-6)	Historical Awareness (Phase 3, Grades 7-9)	Exemplar Appreciation and Critical Analysis (Phases 4 and 5, Grades 10-12)	

Teaching and learning proceed along a continuum from exposure, familiarization, and perceptual training to historical awareness, exemplar appreciation, and critical analysis, stressing discovery and reception learning, didactic coaching, and dialogic teaching methods. Evaluation of aesthetic learning concentrates on the development of aesthetic conceptual maps and the conditions conducive for doing so.

Figure 1. A Cultural Percipience Curriculum (Grades K-12)

ous contexts, certainly more than a course, a year of study, or even three or four years. The process begins early, in the milieu of the family and the community, and continues when young children depart for school and then into later years. In a prototype K-12 curriculum for cultivating cultural percipience, each phase of learning feeds into the next one and helps to inform and energize it. This is what I mean by sequential, cumulative learning.

The basic psychological assumptions pertaining to learning derive largely from cognitive psychology. Four assumptions about cognitive human development are particularly relevant: what is seen and understood is a function of one's conceptual framework (long-term memory, apperceptive mass, and allusionary base), which consists of schemata for understanding; the contents of one's mind are organized hierarchically, which is to say that some ideas are subsumed by others; new information is processed most effectively when it is related to existing schemata; and one's cognitive stock and structure change as the mind assimilates new information. To repeat what has become a commonplace of modern psychology, the image of mind that these principles convey is that of an active, alert, participating, and constructive power. No one in the arts has demonstrated this more conclusively than Rudolf Arnheim and E. H. Gombrich. Yet another principle is that learning in general proceeds along a continuum of accomplishment from simple tasks to more complex and demanding kinds of mastery.

Important consequences for teaching follow. Teachers must respect learners' existing schemata yet insist that learners reach for new levels of mastery and achievement. To do this teachers must not only convey enthusiasm for their subject but, most important, must also have a good grasp of it; otherwise it is difficult to know what should be related to what or why anything is worth doing in the first place. Finally, teachers must have a clear sense of what counts as progress in aesthetic learning.

Teachers who possess no well-developed sense of art themselves can hardly be expected to cultivate a significant sense of art in their students. They will simply pass on their own cultural illiteracy, or the teaching of art will consist primarily of efforts to socialize the young. Such socialization tends to characterize the early years, but even in the later grades attitudes more appropriate for day-care centers and psychological counseling situations are allowed to persist at the expense of the self-discipline needed for formal learning. Self-respect is ensured less through the emotional security afforded by comforting concern than through the accomplishment of specific learning tasks. One teaches subjects, not self-esteem, although the latter may well be a concomitant outcome.

The term *cultural literacy* is now associated with linguistic literacy, spoken and written, and with Hirsch's notion of the extensive curriculum. But art education requires a broader notion of literacy, one that encompasses not only an extensive but also an intensive curriculum and verbal as well as nonverbal forms of apprehension. In this connection, one recalls Levinson's emphasis on sheer listening (chapter 4), on the importance of immersing oneself in works of music in contrast to accumulating a disproportionate amount of discursive knowledge. The same might be said of learning to perceive the nonverbal arts in general. I remember, for instance, my undergraduate courses in art history in which very little reading was assigned, in part because there was not much in the early fifties that instructors considered worth reading but also because one of the aims of the courses was to cultivate visual literacy. Preparation for examinations consisted of reviewing class notes and filling one's mind with as many images as possible. We poured over black-and-white glossy prints that came in little boxes and went through all the reproductions on reserve in the library. Likewise with courses in music appreciation. Guided listening in class and individual listening outside class were emphasized. And it was the shape and expressiveness of art and music that remained long after dates and names were forgotten (although, as someone once said to me, it is rather surprising how much one retains from one's art history courses—or, to put it differently, how much one's allusionary base has been enriched).

On the other hand, the amassing of art-historical knowledge has obvious benefits. Such information may be very helpful in trying to grasp the point of a painting, as is illustrated by Clifton Olds's interpretation of the *St. Luke* painting. According to Hirsch, a little extensive knowledge may go far enough, but a little more, as John Richardson makes clear in his remarks on Constable, lets one see what is really important about certain paintings. Then there are those contexts of dance that Sparshott discusses that are essentially historical in character and require acquaintance with, for example, the evolution of modern dance from classical ballet, and so forth. In other words, knowledge is no handicap to an enjoyment and understanding of the nonverbal arts. I thus take issue with the war on words. As usual, Jacques Barzun has put the matter exactly: "Critical judgment, appreciation, stylistic analysis, disputation about tastes, historical comparisons, and efficient instruction itself depend on the appropriate use of words." In truth, he says, "The benefits of teaching art to the young will consist mainly in the pleasure that comes of being able to see and hear works of art more sharply and subtly, more consciously, to register that pleasure in words, and compare notes with other people similarly inclined." [12] The task is to find the right proportion of words and experience.

I recall the image of a cultural percipience curriculum as an itinerary, a plan for prospective aesthetic sojourners to traverse the world of art with tact and sensitivity. In view of the multinamity of the art world, however, travelers need intelligent and resourceful guides. Traditionally, these guides have been our great critics, Bernard Berenson, Roger Fry, and Kenneth Clark in the visual arts and their counterparts in the other arts. In the schools, such guides are teachers, so let the teacher as art critic be the guide who will prepare learners to be percipient sojourners.

Phase One of Aesthetic Learning:
Perceiving Qualitative Immediacy (K-3)

A humanities interpretation of a cultural percipience curriculum considers outstanding works to be the principal loci of aesthetic qualities. [13] Although aesthetic qualities can be found practically anywhere, they exist in greater abundance, concentration, and intensity in works of art. But because young children have a limited capacity for aesthetic perception, phase one of aesthetic learning should be devoted chiefly to noticing aesthetic qualities in their everyday surroundings and in nature. It is a time for learning to appreciate the qualitative immediacy of things. Qualitative immediacy, as Levi (who follows the writings of Charles Sanders Peirce) puts it, is one of three aspects of reality that, along with dynamic interaction and symbolic meaning, constitute a phenomenology of all that presents itself to human experience.

The perception of qualitative immediacy involves noticing the character of colors, odors, sounds, and tastes, everything that is freshly and vividly present to the senses and that is experienced spontaneously. It is the way, says Levi, the world looked to Adam before he started naming things. In contrast, the notion of dynamic interaction points to the world of relations, including relations of conflict, tension, and confrontation. Perception focuses on action and reaction and movement and strain, the oppositional elements in nature and human life.

Qualitative immediacy and the dynamic relations among things are complemented by the category of symbolic meaning, at least in the broad sense of the term. It takes account of the capacity of objects to refer, point to, or denote something beyond their immediate qualities and relations. Peirce called these moments of awareness of basic aspects of reality—qualitative immediacy, dynamic interaction, and symbolic meaning—"Firstness," "Secondness," and "Thirdness." In works of art, we tend to identify them as aesthetic qualities, formal relations or movements, and meanings. This progression from Firstness to Thirdness will also serve as signposts or markers in the development of aesthetic learning.

Phase one begins by introducing young children to the world of qualitative immediacy by refining whatever sensitivity to immediate qualities they bring with them to school. Whether teachers invite youngsters to notice the qualities of their everyday world, works of art of their own making, or the works of others, including those found in museums or reproduced in books or seen on television, their aim is to foster seeing. Young learners are also brought to realize that works of art are special kinds of objects and performances, museums and concert halls and theaters special places where they are exhibited and performed, and the art world a special segment of society. With such realizations, the young are on their way to becoming percipient art world sojourners. Much of what teachers are already routinely doing in the early years of schooling can be made to serve the cultivation of cultural percipience as understood here. All teachers need is a different attitude and a sense of direction, a realization that what is being done has significance in a larger scheme of purposes and objectives.

What can be added to my previous reflections on arts education is the educational perspective derived from Hirsch's project: teaching selective extensive information about the arts. If, as a humanities-based conception of arts education holds, art may be construed metaphorically as a language and its utterances as artistic statements that must be apprehended appropriately, and if contextual knowledge plays a significant role in aesthetic understanding, then it seems reasonable that there would be a vocabulary to go along with learning an artistic language. Perhaps an analogue are the vocabulary lists that make up a part of the lessons in foreign-language textbooks. In accordance with

Hirsch's notion of cultural literacy, these vocabulary lists would include all those items literate Americans know about the arts—names, events, dates, concepts—as well as additional words pertinent to the tasks entailed by given phases of aesthetic learning. Such a vocabulary will consist of information not only about elite art but also works of popular culture and light entertainment. Such information, Hirsch says, is not necessarily the most highly prized in the culture; it is simply part of the common coin of communication. But some items will be more strategic for achieving the objectives of a particular learning phase. Of course, words should not be taught simply as listings of unrelated items; they should be contextualized and made relevant to objectives.

When one applies to the arts Hirsch's suggestions for cultural literacy in the narrow sense, one can construct a usable vocabulary and publish it in graded materials. Teachers may also consult the *Dictionary of Cultural Literacy* and the graded texts compiled by Hirsch and his colleagues, and they may supplement items with terms of their own. Because specialized terminology plays a necessary role in any subject, no apology is needed for recommending that art teachers use vocabulary lists. Children, Hirsch reminds us, are not really averse to accumulating information.

Phase Two of Aesthetic Learning:
Developing Perceptual Acumen (Grades 4–6)

The word *acumen* in the phrase *perceptual acumen* suggests that phase two of aesthetic learning will stress greater discernment of artistically relevant features of artworks and the contextual knowledge needed for doing so. Consistent with the idea of sequential, cumulative learning, everything learned in phase one gets carried over into phase two and is further developed there. Creative activities continue to be important, but gradually more and more attention is paid to the task of perceiving works of art in their characteristic complexity, particularly works by mature, serious artists.

Although phase one does not discourage students from noticing the various aspects of artworks, it does concentrate on the simple looks, sounds, and feels of things, on the presence of Firstness. Phase two, foundational to what follows, now adds Secondness and Thirdness, the formal and symbolic aspects of artworks. It is a time for more systematic, formal instruction about what to look for and talk about.

Skillful, well-trained teachers are indispensable to phase two. They must be knowledgeable about works of art as stratified objects saturated with feeling and human import that have a capacity to afford a high degree of aesthetic experience. Teachers further should have command of methods appropriate for teaching perception, methods that, instead of being followed inflexibly and mechanically, are simply ways of helping youngsters engage a work and grasp its character. In this respect, Kenneth Clark's description of his own pattern of response to works of art is helpful. His account not only lends itself well to practical application but also enables us to make some important points.[14]

Clark writes of moments of impact, scrutiny, recollection, and renewal. "Impact" refers to the general impression an artwork makes and may be due to practically anything—one of the work's features, a suggestive title perhaps, or even some personal factor idiosyncratic to the percipient. First impressions, however, are often misleading and seldom reveal everything worth seeing. The sensations of initial impact are followed by the activities of close scrutiny, which may involve either a careful inspection of a work's properties and their interrelations or an effort to detect a dominant motive or root idea from which the work derives its overall effect. But it is difficult to sustain aesthetic experience for very long; it must, therefore, alternate with pauses that allow viewers to collect their various senses. The period of scrutiny is followed by one of recollection, during which percipients have recourse to relevant items of knowledge—"nips" of art-historical information, as Clark puts it—that help them see and interpret the work. "Renewal" implies the resumption of the aesthetic experience proper.

The scope of scrutiny, recollection, and renewal is, of course, limited in young learners by their lack of experience and meager stock of knowledge; the same holds for many who teach art. It is the task of instruction to enrich the learner's conceptual framework and allusionary base, to equip long-term memory with necessary skills and knowledge, to thicken the apperceptive mass, and to expand cultural literacy and percipience. Assuming that a decent job of teaching has been done and learners motivated properly, by the end of phase two they should be able to record their impressions of artworks (impact), perform rudimentary formal analysis (scrutiny), call up relevant knowledge and experience (recollection), and rekindle sensory experience (renewal). A method for engaging artworks that Broudy and Ronald Silverman call "aesthetic scanning" could be especially useful for Clark's moments of scrutiny inasmuch as what gets scanned are the sensory, formal, technical, expressive, and symbolic aspects of artworks.[15]

Whatever the preferred terminology or general method, phase-two aesthetic learning emphasizes perceptual training and its prerequisites. Learners extend and elaborate the elementary aesthetic maps they had fashioned in phase one. They become more self-conscious about the perceptual demands made by works of art. Unselfconsciously, they experience those aspects of the aesthetic encounter described in the literature of aesthetics—feelings of being drawn toward and guided by an artwork; free yet disciplined involvement in a work's form, dynamics, and content; discovery of new things and apprehension of familiar things in a new light; and perhaps some sense of personal integration. At least an approximation of mature aesthetic experience can be realized during phase two. As young people's knowledge of and familiarity with art expand and deepen, so do their aesthetic experiences.

In view of Hirsch's notion of cultural literacy, the works selected for perceptual training can be drawn from a broad spectrum of art. A good many of the works should be those that the young are likely to encounter in a national literate culture. Beyond works of this sort, the products of different groups and cultures should also be candidates for selection. Whatever the origin of the works, the preference should be for objects of high quality. What a cultural percipience curriculum adds to Hirsch's extensive curriculum is the methodical teaching of aesthetic skills and the associated vocabulary. Indeed, a cultural percipience curriculum begins to convey intensive information and skills earlier than Hirsch recommends. But learning perceptual skills is not the whole of phase two. Creative activities are still retained, although in the scheme under discussion they diminish in importance as learners pass into phase three.

Phase Three of Aesthetic Learning:
Developing Historical Awareness (Grades 7–9)

Phases one and two of aesthetic learning may be said to have as their major purpose the presentation of art as a special kind of language the statements of which require special knowledge and skills to be understood and enjoyed. In effect, this constitutes teaching what Levi calls the arts of communication. Artistic utterances, however, have a history, and fostering an awareness of art's history constitutes bringing to bear on learning what Levi calls the arts of continuity. Developing a historical sense of art has several objectives: to expand and deepen the learners' cognitive stock and contextual knowledge, to contribute to social cohesion by recalling a common history, and to convey the idea of civilization. In different terms, it is to instill a sense of an art world, a knowledge of art's history, and the beginnings of a theory that enables one not only to define and recognize art but also to understand and appreciate its point. Art history also provides rich sources and pools of metaphor, to recall Gombrich's discussion of general knowledge in chapter 1. In keeping with the image of curriculum as itinerary and the learner as prospective art world sojourner, the study of art history presents the historical landscape of art and its noteworthy monuments.

Aesthetic learning during grades seven through nine occurs within Hirsch's intensive curriculum, leaving the extensive curriculum behind, although there is no good reason for abandoning the study of a relevant vocabulary. Students should now possess a national literate vocabulary about the arts, acquired in the previous phases of learning as well as relevant schemata for viewing works of art. And they are capable of taking what Sparshott called an art stance toward works of art. Important to remember is that phases one and two, especially phase two, are prerequisite to studying art historically. Young people need a sense of what art is before undertaking a survey of the different forms it has taken from the caves to the present, before they add more information, knowledge, and experience to their cognitive stock and allusionary base. Again, this goes far beyond Hirsch's notion of cultural literacy and contributes to what I term "cultural percipience."

Another justification for studying the history of art—in addition, that is, to expanding and enriching the cognitive stock of learners and building a progressively more inclusive sense of art—is the awareness of civilization it conveys. This reason was featured in the report on arts education titled *Toward Civilization*.[16] Art history is to be accorded high significance as a record of the wondrous ways in which the human mind has imposed form on matter, created order out of disorder, and helped shaped civilization. Through precious images, memorable sounds, and unforgettable words, works of art reveal how humankind has evolved from a brutal state of raw nature to a state of human freedom in which the creation of artistic values has become of paramount importance, ranking behind only the promotion of intellectual and moral values. Put another way, outstanding works of art are aesthetic records of heroic attempts to achieve culture and civilization. Despite the efforts of social scientists to define culture more broadly, we keep coming back to the associations of the term with excellence and high culture. To be sure, the history of art memorializes not only humanity's proud attainments but also its instances of inhumanity, although it usually does the latter in order to warn about the fragility of culture and civilization and to recall humanistic values when irrationality and barbarism threaten to gain the upper hand. Finally, art history teaches appreciation of the role of tradition, in particular its persistence and continuity. Gombrich laments the loss of tradition, and Hirsch likewise finds it intolerably attenuated in young people.

Thus, the study of art history is immediately enjoyable and has different kinds of instrumental values. But whereas teaching in phases one and two permits a degree of informality—one is, after all, working with very young children—phase-three instruction is by necessity systematic and formal. The history of art is not something to be toyed with. It exacts a degree of discipline and sustained attention over a period of time. Practical activities need not be eliminated, but they should be related to the development of historical awareness.

Regarding Hirsch's emphasis on specificity, phase three poses no special difficulties. The history of art is what the standard texts say it is, that is, what Janson, Gardner, Gombrich, Honour and Fleming, and others say it is. These art history books vary in the amount and types of information they convey and in level of reading difficulty, but it is this kind of art history that I have in mind for phase three.[17] Some histories of art are now available in texts suitable for young learners, although knowledgeable teachers will find their own ways of conveying such material.

The standard histories of art stress Western art history, but not exclusively so; the Honour and Fleming text, for example, has sections on Asian and African art. But for American students it is only natural that a study of the Western cultural heritage should be prominent in developing a sense of art. This is not to say that earlier phases of learning lack a multicultural dimension, and phase five will consist in part of comparative studies of Western and non-Western works. But even the Western cultural tradition contains more than a little cultural variance as well as numerous points of contact and intercultural influence between Western and non-Western societies.

What is further needed to overcome the state of cultural amnesia in contemporary education is a survey of art history that stresses the chronology of major periods and their characteristic works. Matters have deteriorated to the point that even college graduates have but a slight notion of what happened when. Young learners should also come to appreciate the facts of continuity and change in artistic traditions, to know how things got started, got carried along, and gradually changed. Perhaps, to use pedagogical jargon, advance organizers could be written along the lines of Gombrich's creed for Western civilization—one for the whole period to be spanned over three years (grades 7–9) and one for each year of study. Just as a good tour guide does in planning a sensible itinerary, the teacher could mark out and provide a glimpse of major points of interest before embarking for particular destinations. Although phase-three learning would not stop there, such synopses could go a long way toward satisfying the demands of cultural literacy in the narrow sense of the term. True, a survey of the arts would not permit prolonged study of any particular work. But considering that three years of middle schooling have been allotted to the history of art, it should be possible to accomplish something worthwhile in that much time—if, that is, a portion of what now constitutes arts education can be reorganized and the rest relegated to extracurricular activities.

To shore up a defense of studying Western art at a time when Western values are under attack, I will argue once again that the Western cultural heritage is the preeminent (although not the only) tradition of American civilization. Its study precedes the study of other civilizations and confers the right to criticize it. Such statements seem so commonsensical that one can but wonder at the current state of an intellectual community that rejects them. But reflection about educational objectives has always been subject to dramatic swings of opinion, and perhaps there is some reassurance in the fact that Americans typically shun extremist thinking. Perhaps the political upheavals of recent years will persuade a new generation that Western political and cultural traditions are not so oppressive after all and that cultural unity and harmony are preferable to cultural particularism and separatism.

Phase Four of Aesthetic Learning:
Exemplar Appreciation (Grades 10–11)

Ideally, by the time students reach grades 10 and 11 they have been sensitized to the qualitative immediacy of life and the ways works of art manifest interrelations of sensory, formal, technical, expressive, and symbolic properties. They have further learned that works of art are typically housed, preserved, exhibited, and enjoyed in cultural institutions of the art world and that art has a history of outstanding accomplishment. Along the way they have learned a vocabulary that goes with talking about, understanding, and enjoying art, a vocabulary comprised of items from Hirsch's lexicon of cultural literacy and additional items required for studying art in some depth. The warnings of Hirsch and other educational theorists about the limitations of educational formalism have thus been heeded, and learners have come to appreciate the uses of specific information and knowledge. They also have realized that creative and performing skills alone are insufficient for effective communication, for cultural literacy or cultural percipience. Young people have, in Hirsch's terms, traveled through the extensive curriculum to the intensive one, all in the service of building a well-developed sense of art.

Becoming culturally percipient thus requires cultivating more than one frame of mind, more than one type of intelligence. It cannot consist solely of the artistic intelligence involved in working in the material of a medium. Nor does the identification of different types of intelligence mandate a division of schooling into subjects each of which would specialize in one form of intelligence. I emphasize this to register my disagreement with the belief of theorists who assert that creative activities should be the cornerstone of arts education.[18] Such activities are enjoyable and important instrumentally in cultivating cultural percipience but are hardly the whole or the most important part of becoming culturally percipient. The conviction that the products of art can be understood only through knowing the details of its crafting or making has even been called the professional's fallacy. In truth, it is possible to learn far more about art's distinctive character and functions from studying art history than from studio courses. Too much cultural knowledge is sacrificed in the latter in time-consuming attempts to master technique. It is thus the art stance taken toward works of art, not the making of artworks, that is featured in a humanities-based curriculum for arts education. To develop competence in this stance, aesthetic, historical, and philosophical frames of mind are required, all those mental activities implicit in Levi's arts of communication, continuity, and criticism, plus creation.

Students should now be ready to undertake the study of selected masterworks for purposes of appreciation in the proper sense of the word—the valuing and admiration of some of the finest forms of human accomplishment. This is important because with the loss of a sense of tradition we have also lost respect for individual achievement and excellence to the point where "excellence" has become pejoratively associated with elitism. The denigration of excellence has in turn contributed to the vulgarization of both high and popular culture. Max Lerner, in the second edition of his monumental *America as a Civilization*, claims that America lacks neither energy nor talent. "Where it is lacking is in judgment and prudence. . . . Its high arts as well as its popular culture revel in obsessions and excesses. The true danger it runs, as a collective organism, are not of a spent senility but of the turmoils of adolescence." [19]

In its focus on exemplar appreciation, phase-four aesthetic learning does not leave historical knowledge or anything else behind, but the emphasis is less on coverage than on the intensive study of a few works, on concentrated viewing, listening, and reading. In important respects this phase represents a culmination of the first three phases. The aim is to learn to appreciate works that, by virtue of their resplendent form and content, have earned a permanent place in human history as sources of perennially fresh experience and aesthetic wisdom. At a time when pessimism abounds regarding the ability of individuals and nations to solve their problems, when nihilism reigns in cultural studies, and new determinisms (really revived older, discredited ones) deny the potency of ideas and individual will, it is necessary to recall peaks of human excellence. Humankind needs to be reminded of what has been done in order to envision what may still be possible. The emphasis in phase-four aesthetic learning on intensive viewing, listening, and reading does not mean separating a work from its historical context, but care should be taken to ensure that contextual knowledge is used with the sole aim of discovering the excellences of a work. This is contextualism par excellence.

The demand for curricular specificity is once again easy to meet. Acknowledged masterworks are key objects of study. Perceptual skills and knowledge of the place of great works in the history of art will already have been gained in earlier phases of learning. It is helpful, moreover, to return to a work that was discussed previously and make it the object of greater attention. In this regard, an especially helpful text for teachers is F. David Martin and Lee Jacobus's *The Humanities through the Arts.*[20] In addition to exploring individual works in this phase, complexes or aggregations of works would also be suitable for study—for example, the Acropolis in Athens, the Giotto frescoes of Padua, the sculpture and architecture of the Sistine Chapel, the painters of the High Renaissance, the cubism of Braque and Picasso, the abstract expressionism of de Kooning and Kline, and so forth.

Elsewhere I have discussed at some length the nature of excellence in art and will here refer only briefly to that discussion.[21] The peculiar excellence of art lies in the capacity that its best instances possess to energize experience in distinctive, worthwhile ways. Experience so energized is often called aesthetic experience, which is a satisfactory definition so long as the notion of aesthetic experience is kept comprehensive enough to accommodate the symbolic aspect of artworks as well as their sensory, formal, and expressive properties. If this is done, then an excellent work of art is one that has a high capacity to induce aesthetic experience. Standard history of art texts are full of reproductions of such works.[22]

Among volumes that are helpful less for detailed discussions of aesthetic experience than for identifying the marks of excellence in artworks is Jakob Rosenberg's *On Quality in Art: Criteria of Excellence, Past and Present.*[23] Rosenberg compares a number of master drawings and prints by major and minor artists from the fifteenth century to the twentieth, and it comes as no surprise that the quality of formal organization ranks highly in both representational and nonrepresentational works of art. In addition, major works of art exhibit inventiveness, originality, suggestiveness, and economy and reveal sensitivity, articulateness, consistency, selectiveness, vitality, range of accents, intensity, expressiveness, and a feeling for the medium. The selection of such qualities as indicators of aesthetic worth does not reflect merely Rosenberg's preferences, but those of aesthetically intelligent observers generally. In *Past, Present, East and West,* Sherman E. Lee notes similar criteria of excellence in Chinese painting; he mentions the qualities of suppleness, liveliness, variety, and individualism as well as a work's formal organization that fuses medium, design, subject, and meaning.[24]

Perhaps the best single source accessible to nonspecialists is Kenneth Clark's *What Is a Masterpiece?*[25] What, asks Clark, do such works as Giotto's *Lamentation over the Dead Christ,* Raphael's *School of Athens,* Rubens's *Descent from the Cross,* Courbet's *Funeral of Ornans,* and Picasso's *Guernica* have in common? Each painting fills the imagination and expresses deep and complex emotions while revealing supreme artistry in its masterly form and finality of design. Most important, each work reveals the remaking of traditional ideas and forms in order to render them expressive of the artist and of the times in which the artist lived, all the while retaining a significant link with the past. When there is an important story to tell, especially a tragic one, a work gains in potential for filling the imagination. Moreover, excellence of the highest order impresses by a profound commitment to human values and insight into the human condition—"the quest for truth," as Broudy called it. Like Rosenberg and Lee, Clark locates the excellence of masterpieces in their inspired virtuosity, supreme compositional power, intensity of feeling, masterful design, uncompromising integrity, imaginative force, originality of vision, and, again, profound sense of human values.

Major contemporary works often reveal the same range of qualities as traditional masterpieces, and some observers speculate that films will be the masterpieces of the twentieth century. Yet given the commercial constraints on filmmaking perhaps the most we can expect from motion pictures are what Martin S. Dworkin has called "fine failures." Stanley Kauffmann has also remarked that, in talking about film, the term *classic* must be hedged in with qualifications. Still, in principle, films are capable of achieving excellence, and when they do, Kauffmann observes, they tend to be rated better or poorer because of their satisfying or failing to meet traditional criteria of excellence: inventiveness, imaginative energy, dramatic content, technical competence, and—germane to the medium—dialogue and dramatization, successful transformation of literary into cinematic values, psychological complexity, and spiritual power.[26]

Summarizing the kinds of justification that can be given for praising works of art, Harold Osborne concludes that we value certain works for three major reasons: strictly artistic reasons, which implies artistic virtuosity in the completed product; the capacity to provide aesthetic satisfaction in a responsive beholder; and stature, which refers to the ways works of art perform a number of subsidiary (at least Osborne thinks they are subsidiary) functions such as providing understanding, presenting nonverbal thought, and expressing embodied feeling. Nelson Goodman, on the other hand, would make understanding the primary function of art—although it is not obvious that we always go to works of art for understanding.[27]

As Sherman Lee's remarks about Chinese painting indicate, excellence in art can be found in all civilizations. Even in societies where art seems to perform a strictly practical or ceremonial function there are often standards of artistic judgment, excellence, and appreciation that can be detected, as H. Gene Blocker has shown in *The Aesthetics of Primitive Art*.[28] And so, although it is to be expected that two years of exemplar appreciation during phase four will include the study of masterpieces from the Western tradition, this is also the time for some comparative studies of Western and non-Western works (Asian, African, and Central American, for example). Such studies are also consistent with the entertaining of alternatives, one of the objectives of humanities education. Culturally percipient persons would be less than liberal in their outlook if they had no familiarity with the art of other cultures and did not understand the point of it. Put another way, awareness of some of the arts of different societies should be part of any well-developed sense of art. Teaching about non-Western art should not be undertaken for political reasons. The objective is to contribute importantly to young people's general education and to enable them to live more meaningful lives.

Although I have taught history courses in non-Western art, my knowledge of it is still limited, and so I am somewhat reluctant to make specific suggestions. However, one kind of comparative study I found helpful uses the method of paired comparisons such as those found in Benjamin Rowland's *Art in East and West: An Introduction through Comparisons*.[29] Would that similar volumes were available on African and Western art and Latin American and Western art. Rowland points out both the similarities and differences among the works selected from various historical periods in each of the civilizations he discusses. His emphasis is not on historical analysis so much as on the appreciation of the aesthetic values of the works and the practices and traditions that produced them. The works paired for comparison are similar in subject matter and presentation, for example, human figures, portraits, religious images, landscapes, birds, animals, and flowers.

Rowland's introduction distinguishes traditional from nontraditional art (the latter begins with the individualism of the Renaissance) and explains that works will be discussed in regard to their style, iconography, and technique. He does not attempt to show the cultural influence of one civilization on another or confer validity on contemporary artists whose works reflect the influence of non-Western traditional art. Rather, he states that the comparisons "illustrate accidental parallels in the art of the East and West, stemming from a common background or affected by similar circumstances, social, artistic, and technical, in the process of their making." The discussion of paired works "is intended to point out the aesthetic properties peculiar to the Eastern and Western points of view toward art and to show how parallel artistic climates inevitably produce a peculiar kind of expression appropriate to its moment and place in art history" (vii). This kind of comparative analysis has the virtue of satisfying the humanistic objective of addressing differences among cultures at the same time that it indicates parallels and similarities, which is a contribution to an understanding of civilization. Published at a time when advocates of difference were less assertive than they now are, Rowland's analysis can be read as a needed response to the writings of multicultural extremists.

Rowland's distinction between traditional and nontraditional artworks is also worth noting. It stresses the practical utility and symbolic function of the former, for example, as revelations of supernatural powers that govern over the terrestrial order.

> In a traditional art, whether we are concerned with portraits, landscapes, religious images, or birds and animals, the artist's point of view is never realistic, but conceptual, in that he intends to represent the most essential or typical aspects of things as the mind knows them, rather than as the eye sees them. The aim is to represent a universal and recognizable symbol, rather than a facsimile of an actual object. It is not only permissible but necessary to draw a head in profile with an eye in full-face, because these are the most characteristic aspects of these features. In portraying a river landscape the traditional artist may be expected to represent the stream by a series of wavy lines. The fishes in the water would be drawn in profile, and the birds above it with their wings outspread, because these are the attitudes that everyone recognizes as the most typical of fishes and birds. (2)

Regarding nontraditional art:

> Whereas traditional art is almost invariably anonymous, and the painter or sculptor a dedicated craftsman, the nontraditional artist is an individual who uses art as an expression of his own personal moods or as a means for displaying his own technical virtuosity. In nontraditional periods artists will express themselves in realistic terms because their whole belief and experience are centered on the material world. The term, nontraditional art, is usually assigned to all work beginning with the Renaissance in Europe when the artist strove to record the outward appearances of nature rather than the underlying spirit operating behind the facade of actuality. (2)

Even those Eastern works that appear to be naturalistic are often traditional because their creators were more concerned to suggest the inner
life and vitality of the subject than their realistic outward appearances.
Among the thirty-one pairs that Rowland discusses are a Greek statue
of Apollo and an Indian Jain Tirthankara; a portrait of Charles VII of
France by Jean Fouquet and one of a Japanese military leader, Mina-
moto no Yoritomo, by Fujiwara no Takanobu; and a landscape by the
American painter John Marin and one by a Chinese painter of the Zen
sect of Buddhism.

Another volume, this time by an anthropologist, Jacques Maquet, is
interesting for its discussion of the universal as well as the culturally
unique characteristics of the arts of different civilizations. *The Aesthetic
Experience: An Anthropologist Looks at the Arts* is also noteworthy for its
use of Western aesthetic theory, namely, Harold Osborne's, to discuss
the aesthetic qualities of artworks.[30] Well illustrated, the text ranges over
discussions of works from Western, Asian, African, and Latin American
civilizations. The volume, although written from a different perspective,
is an excellent complement to Rowland's book. To supplement the views
from art history and anthropology, Blocker's philosophical discussion
in *The Aesthetics of Primitive Art* can also be recommended, and Thomas
Munro's *Oriental Aesthetics* makes a strong argument for the increased
use of comparative studies.[31] I repeat that a humanities-based arts education is not a single discipline; it is neither art history, aesthetics, nor
anthropology. Rather, it draws on these disciplines and others in trying
to achieve educational objectives.

I recommend a multicultural dimension for arts education at this
stage of aesthetic development not in obeisance to extreme multiculturalists but in an attempt to realize one of the important objectives of
humanistic education, the study of alternative modes of life and expression. Multicultural thinking, as I suggested in chapter 4, occasions three
abuses: dogmatic multiculturalism, which presumes the superiority of
one's own culture; multicultural aestheticism, which simply scans the
superficial aspects and appearances of artworks; and political multiculturalism, which advances the interests of special groups. In contrast,
dialectical multiculturalism is the only kind worthy of liberal learning.

The contemporary situation in intellectual life and education makes it
necessary to repeat that in several phases of learning, certainly in phases
one and two and to a certain extent in three, four, and five, works by
members of different ethnic groups and artists of either gender can serve
as objects of instruction. The aims of phases one and two—exposure,

familiarization, and perceptual training—can be promoted through the use of works by artists from all sorts of cultural backgrounds. There will, of course, be fewer opportunities for such diversity in phase three, which concentrates on the dominant tradition. Major works by women, however, can be candidates for study in phase four, and topics in seminars devoted to critical analysis may likewise feature a broad spectrum of concerns expressed by different groups.

Phase Five of Aesthetic Learning: Critical Analysis (Grade 12)

When the goals of society are obvious to its members and in little need of explanation and the functions of art are similarly transparent, the need to think clearly and systematically about the arts and society is not as pressing as it is when confusion exists on both counts. Given the developments in the art world over the last century and a half, especially since mid-twentieth century, the nature, meaning, value, and function of art have all become problematic. The loss of a common context for responding to art has resulted in an art public that tends, with rare exception, to withhold judgment and acquiesce in whatever is done in the name of art, however trivial, outrageous, and perverse.

The uneven quality of discussion and the failure of a genuine debate to emerge regarding a number of recent controversial events in the art world are ample testimony to our inability to think critically about art and what we expect from it and want from artists. What are young people to think, for example, when their elders and teachers are incapable of discussing the relative value of such art world happenings as the desecration of the American flag in an exhibition at a major art institute; a photograph showing a crucifix immersed in a jar containing the artist's urine; the display by an acclaimed photographer of photographs said to be pornographic; the disruption of pedestrian traffic by a commissioned sculpture and subsequent public demands for the sculpture's removal; self-mutilation touted as art; and (my favorite) the sponsoring by an art institute of naked artists duelling ritualistically in cow dung. (Eaton's example was an artwork consisting of parts of slaughtered horses placed in jars). My point is not to take easy advantage of these incidents, but to ask how they came to be taken for art and what we need to know about art in order to make defensible judgments about them. Or in a democracy do we believe that works of art are above judgment?

A student in one of my classes was teaching an advanced placement course in art history in a Chicago suburban high school at the time when the controversy exploded over a work in a student exhibition at the art school of the Chicago Art Institute. The work was so arranged as to invite viewers to walk across an American flag (spread on the floor) in order to record their opinions in a book provided for the purpose, which apparently some viewers did. My reason for mentioning this is not to recount the aftermath of strong reaction and public opinion but to report that in addition to the high school students wanting to know what their teacher (my student) thought about the matter, they also wanted to know what their teacher's teacher thought, that is, what I thought.

My response was along the lines of what I have been arguing about general knowledge and cultural percipience: Without a sufficient context for responding to art, it is difficult to know how to handle such happenings when they are thrust upon us. And one builds such a context by learning more about art, more about its history, theory, and outstanding cultural monuments. Only then is one is in a position to decide whether to extend the status of art to works that challenge well-known instances of it. Otherwise, one is at the mercy of artists' whims, of special interests, and of the judgments of people like the impresario who said that it was the aim of his performances to vaporize the mind by bombing the senses.[32]

A senior seminar is the place for gaining perspective on controversial topics and issues in the arts and for providing adolescents with opportunities to develop their own ideas about art. By this time learners will have enough perceptual acumen, historical awareness, and appreciation of excellence in art to participate in critical analysis and discussion. It is not the case that critical thinking has been avoided up to this point, but it is only now that learners are in a position to become adept at it. I use "critical thinking" rather loosely as backing up one's statements with good reasons and entertaining the reasons and judgments of others, in short, as reasoned discourse.

Topics suitable for a senior seminar are not hard to come by. Because getting to the heart of a discipline is often said to require becoming clear about its characteristic criteria of judgment, a senior seminar might well address the problems of the critical evaluation of art, for which the writings of art critics and the analyses of aestheticians would be helpful resources. Other topics are available from *Puzzles about Art: An Aesthetics Casebook* by Margaret P. Battin et al.[33] The puzzles in this book feature problems in defining art, beauty, and aesthetic experience, meaning and interpretation, creativity, extra-artistic values, and critical judgment. My experience has been that students enjoy reading and thinking about conundrums that are not only intriguing in themselves but can also have genuine relevance for understanding art. By the senior year, then, students will have well-stocked conceptual frameworks, and Hirsch's complaint that attempts to teach critical thinking are frustrated by a lack of specific knowledge should have lost some of its force.

By the end of phase five, students will ideally possess a well-developed sense of art that enables them to traverse the art world with a fair degree of cultural percipience, the latter being an expanded notion of Hirsch's cultural literacy. This is the overarching goal of a humanities-based interpretation of arts education. Teaching art as a humanity implies bringing to bear on the teaching of art the arts of creation, communication, continuity, and criticism, whose associated disciplines are artistic making, art history, art criticism, and aesthetics (the philosophy of art). Appropriately embodied in a sequential program of five phases that stresses cumulative learning, a cultural percipience curriculum features the teaching of both specific content and general skills. Because of the tendency to associate the term *literacy* with verbal literacy, with written and spoken language, I have used the expression *cultural percipience*, which implies finesse in matters of understanding art and culture. I have often referred to arts education and of the nature of percipient viewing, listening, and reading, but by and large my examples have been taken from the visual arts, which I know best. I think, however, that with appropriate qualifications the interpretation of cultural literacy presented here has broad applicability.

In *Art Education: A Critical Necessity*, Levi and I assumed that both art and art education are critical necessities. But how can that be, when art is so generally regarded as a luxury and enjoyed only during one's leisure? Certainly many of those who launch national educational reform movements do not think the arts are critical necessities. Yet the fulfillments and satisfactions that derive from experiencing major works of art are ingredients in any worthwhile life. A healthy society is one that provides its members with physical and spiritual amenities, including a diet of art that nourishes the human mind and emotions and provides a sense of common values. In *Aesthetics and the Good Life*, a work that returns the philosophy of art to its classical concerns, Marcia Eaton, whose observations about cultural literacy were discussed in chapter 4, writes that one of her objectives was to show "that part of what it means to lead a moral and rational life is to respond aesthetically to objects, events, and other people. Having aesthetic experiences is thus one of life's central goals." Indeed, "aesthetic activities and responses enrich life and provide . . . 'delight' not only by providing pleasure but by sensitizing, vitalizing, and inspiring human beings."[34] If the study of art can do these things, then arts education is a critical necessity. It should be part of the general knowledge that a program of general education conveys in the schools.

Notes

Chapter 1: The Tradition of General Knowledge

1. E. H. Gombrich, "The Tradition of General Knowledge" in *Ideals and Idols: Essays on Values in History and Art* (New York: E. P. Dutton, 1979).

2. Gombrich, "The Tradition of General Knowledge," 11; subsequent references to specific pages will be given in the text.

3. Erwin Panofsky, *Meaning in the Visual Arts* (1955; repr. Chicago: University of Chicago Press, 1982), 324.

4. Gombrich, "The Tradition of General Knowledge," 18; subsequent references to specific pages will be given in the text.

Chapter 2: Hirsch on Cultural Literacy

1. C. P. Snow, *The Two Cultures and the Scientific Revolution* (New York: Cambridge University Press, 1959), and R. A. Smith, "The Two Cultures Debate Today," *Oxford Review of Education* 4, no. 3 (1978): 257–65.

2. R. A. Smith, *Excellence in Art Education: Ideas and Initiatives*, rev. ed. (Reston: National Art Education Association, 1987).

3. This tendency is commonplace knowledge among arts educators, but it was confirmed in John Goodlad's *A Place Called School* (New York: McGraw Hill, 1984). Goodlad observes that there is far too much emphasis on creative and performing activities in programs of arts education at the expense of the study of works as cultural objects (220).

4. *Academic Preparation in the Arts* (New York: The College Board, 1985).

The report states that significant progress should be made in the development of three kinds of abilities: "1. Knowledge of how to produce or perform works of art. 2. Knowledge of how to analyze, interpret, and evaluate artworks. 3. Knowledge of artworks of other periods and cultures and their contexts" (20). But the report is silent on which artworks, periods, cultures, and contexts. In *Perplexing Dreams: Is There a Core Tradition in the Humanities?* (Washington: American Council of Learned Societies, 1987), Roger Shattuck expresses similar dissatisfaction with the College Board's earlier report, *Academic Preparation for College: What Students Need to Know and Be Able to Do* (1983): "In science and mathematics, the booklet describes fairly well-defined content requirements. In the humanities (English, the arts, and foreign languages) the emphasis falls entirely on what I call 'empty skills'—to read, to write, to analyze, to describe, to evaluate. To what specifics or context are these skills to be applied?" (3).

5. Jerome S. Bruner, *The Process of Education* (1960; repr. Cambridge: Harvard University Press, 1977), with new preface.

6. See Smith, *Excellence in Art Education*, chap. 5.

7. Allan Bloom, *The Closing of the American Mind: How Higher Education Has Failed Democracy and Impoverished the Souls of Today's Students* (New York: Simon and Schuster, 1987).

8. E. D. Hirsch, Jr., "Cultural Literacy," *The American Scholar* 52 (Spring 1983): 159–69; subsequent references to specific pages will be given in the text.

9. I refer principally to the writings of Howard Gardner. See, for example, his "Toward More Effective Arts Education," in *Aesthetics and Arts Education*, ed. Ralph A. Smith and Alan Simpson (Urbana: University of Illinois Press, 1991), 281.

10. E. D. Hirsch, Jr., *Cultural Literacy* (1987; repr. New York: Random House, 1988); subsequent references to specific pages will be given in the text.

11. Gunnar Myrdal, *An American Dilemma* (New York: McGraw Hill, 1964), 1:3–50.

12. Quoted by Arch Puddington in "Clarence Thomas and the Blacks," *Commentary* 93 (February 1992): 29.

13. Jeff Smith, "Cultural Literacy and the Academic 'Left,'" *National Forum* 29 (Summer 1989): 21.

14. Smith, "Cultural Literacy," 21.

15. Elizabeth Fox-Genovese, "The Feminist Challenge to the Canon," *National Forum* 69 (Summer 1989): 33, 34.

16. In this connection, see D. H. Perkins and Gavriel Saloman, "Are Cognitive Skills Context-Bound?" *Educational Researcher* 18 (January–February 1989): 16–25, and Edy S. Quellmaetz, "Developing Reasoning Skills," in *Teaching Thinking Skills: Theory and Practice*, ed. Joan Boykoff and Robert J. Sternberg (New York: W. H. Freeman, 1987), 86–105. I am grateful to Elizabeth Goldsmith-Conley for pointing out these discussions.

Chapter 3: The Reception of *Cultural Literacy*

1. Stanley Aronowitz and Henry A. Giroux, *Postmodern Education: Politics, Culture, and Social Criticism* (Minneapolis: University of Minnesota Press, 1991), 26; subsequent references to specific pages will be given in the text.

2. E. D. Hirsch, *Cultural Literacy* (1987; repr. New York: Random House, 1988), 130.

3. Gerald Graff and William E. Cain, "Peace Plan for the Canon Wars," *National Forum* 69 (Summer 1989): 8.

4. Lionel Trilling, *The Liberal Imagination* (1950; repr. New York: Harcourt Brace Jovanovich, 1979), preface.

5. Richard Hofstadter, *Anti-intellectualism in American Life* (New York: Alfred A. Knopf, 1963), 29.

6. Robert Scholes, "Aiming a Canon at the Curriculum," *Salamagundi* 72 (Fall 1986): 101–17.

7. Scholes, "Aiming a Canon," 106.

8. William Bennett, " 'To Reclaim a Legacy': Text of a Report on Humanities in Education," *Chronicle of Higher Education*, 28 November 1984, 16–21.

9. E. D. Hirsch, " 'Cultural Literacy' Does Not Mean a 'Canon,' " *Salamagundi* 72 (Fall 1986): 119–20; emphasis in the original.

10. See, for example, Richard C. Anderson et al., *Becoming a Nation of Readers: The Report of the National Commission on Reading* (Washington, D.C.: The National Institute of Education, 1985).

11. Jacques Barzun, *The House of Intellect* (New York: Harper and Brothers, 1959), vii.

12. George Steiner, "Little-Read Schoolhouse," *The New Yorker*, 1 June 1987, 106–10.

13. Christopher Clausen, "It Is Not Elitist to Place Major Literature at the Center of a Curriculum, *Chronicle of Higher Education*, 13 January 1988, 1952.

14. Roger Shattuck, *Perplexing Dreams: Is There a Core Tradition in the Humanities?* (Washington: American Council of Learned Societies, 1987), 7.

15. Bertrand de Jouvenal, *The Art of Conjecture*, translated by Nikita Lary (New York: Basic Books, 1967), 251–56.

16. The entire debate from Snow's point of view, including the reprinting of the original essay, Snow's second look, his response to Leavis, and further reflections, can be found in Snow's *Public Affairs* (New York: Scribner's, 1971). Cf. Roger Scruton, "Modern Philosophy and the Neglect of Aesthetics," *Times Literary Supplement*, 7 June 1987, 604, 616–17, and R. A. Smith, *The Sense of Art* (New York: Routledge, 1989), 146–56.

17. Hirsch writes a syndicated weekly column for newspapers that discusses in more detail some of the items on his word list.

Chapter 4: The Arts and Contextual Knowledge

1. The implementation of Hirsch's ideas about cultural literacy is being assisted by the Core Knowledge Foundation (formerly Cultural Literacy Foundation) located in Charlottesville, Virginia, and headed by Hirsch. The foundation publishes a newsletter, *Common Knowledge*, which keeps those interested abreast of a range of activities, including efforts to establish a core knowledge curriculum in schools.

Among the publications discussed in the newsletter, in addition to *Cultural Literacy* (1988), are *The Dictionary of Cultural Literacy: What Every American Needs to Know* (1988), edited by Hirsch, Joseph F. Kett, and James Trefil, and *A First Dictionary of Cultural Literacy* (1989), which is aimed at the elementary grades. Hirsch is also editing a Core Knowledge Series that consists of graded texts, for example, *What Your First Grader Needs to Know, Your Second Grader,* and so forth, through six grades. Also available from the foundation are a general information brochure, an idea book for interested schools, a parents' guide to core knowledge, and cultural literacy tests for the different grades.

2. Ralph A. Smith, ed., *Cultural Literacy and Arts Education* (Urbana: University of Illinois Press, 1991); subsequent references to specific pages will be given in the text.

3. E. D. Hirsch, Jr., "Reflections about Cultural Literacy and Arts Education," in *Cultural Literacy and Arts Education*, ed. Ralph A. Smith (Urbana: University of Illinois Press, 1991), 1–6.

4. Peter Winch, "Text and Context" in *Trying to Make Sense* (New York: Basil Blackwell, 1987), 18–32.

5. Francis Sparshott, "Contexts of Dance," in *Cultural Literacy and Arts Education*, ed. Ralph A. Smith (Urbana: University of Illinois Press, 1991), 73–87; subsequent references to specific pages will be given in the text.

6. This is the theme of my book *The Sense of Art* (New York: Routledge, 1989).

7. Henry Aiken, "Learning and Teaching in the Arts," *Journal of Aesthetic Education* 5 (October 1971): 39–67.

8. Jerrold Levinson, "Musical Literacy," in *Cultural Literacy and Arts Education*, ed. Ralph A. Smith (Urbana: University of Illinois Press, 1991), 15–30; subsequent references to specific pages will be given in the text.

9. Patti P. Gillespie, "Theater Education and Hirsch's Contextualism: How Do We Get There, and Do We Want to Go?" in *Cultural Literacy and Arts Education*, ed. Ralph A. Smith (Urbana: University of Illinois Press, 1991), 31–47; subsequent references to specific pages will be given in the text.

10. Marcia Muelder Eaton, "Context, Criticism, and Art Education: Putting Meaning into the Life of Sisyphus," in *Cultural Literacy and Arts Education*, ed.

Ralph A. Smith (Urbana: University of Illinois Press, 1991), 97–110; subsequent references to specific pages will be given in the text.

11. Ronald Berman, "Cultural History and Cultural Materialism," in *Cultural Literacy and Arts Education*, ed. Ralph A. Smith (Urbana: University of Illinois Press, 1991), 111–21; subsequent references to specific pages will be given in the text.

12. John Richardson, "The Visual Arts and Cultural Literacy," in *Cultural Literacy and Arts Education*, ed. Ralph A. Smith (Urbana: University of Illinois Press, 1991), 51–72, subsequent references to specific pages will be given in the text; John Richardson, *Art: The Way It Is*, 3d ed. (Englewood Cliffs: Prentice-Hall, 1986), 12.

13. Clifton Olds, "Jan Gossaert's *St. Luke Painting the Virgin*," in *Cultural Literacy and Arts Education*, ed. Ralph A. Smith (Urbana: University of Illinois Press, 1991), 89–96; subsequent references to specific pages will be given in the text.

14. Walter Clark, Jr., "Literature, Education, and Cultural Literacy," in *Cultural Literacy and Arts Education*, ed. Ralph A. Smith (Urbana: University of Illinois Press, 1991), 49–56; subsequent references to specific pages will be given in the text.

15. Michael J. Parsons, "Aesthetic Literacy: The Psychological Context," in *Cultural Literacy and Arts Education*, ed. Ralph A. Smith (Urbana: University of Illinois Press, 1991), 135–46.

16. Michael J. Parsons, *How We Understand Art: A Cognitive Developmental Account of Aesthetic Experience* (New York: Cambridge University Press, 1987). Cf. Smith, *The Sense of Art*, 117–23.

17. David Elliott, "Music as Culture: Toward a Multicultural Concept of Arts Education," in *Cultural Literacy and Arts Education*, ed. Ralph A. Smith (Urbana: University of Illinois Press, 1991), 147–66; subsequent references to specific pages will be given in the text.

18. Israel Scheffler, "Making and Understanding," in *In Praise of the Cognitive Emotions* (New York: Routledge, 1991), 41, quoted in Elliott, "Music as Culture," 158.

19. Richard Pratte, *Pluralism in Education* (Springfield, Ill.: Charles C. Thomas, 1979).

Chapter 5: The Question of Multiculturalism

1. Roger Kimball, *Tenured Radicals* (New York Harper and Row, 1991), 194.

2. R. A. Smith, "Celebrating the Arts in Their Cultural Diversity: Some Wrong and Right Ways to Do It," in *Arts in Cultural Diversity*, ed. Jack Condous,

Janterie Howlett, and John Skull (New York: Holt, Rinehart and Winston, 1980), 82–88, and "Forms of Multicultural Education in the Arts," *Journal of Multi-cultural and Cross-cultural Research in Art Education* 1 (Fall 1983): 23–32.

3. For a brief summary of INSEA's origins, see Edwin Ziegfeld, "Notes on Its History," *Journal of Aesthetic Education* 12 (April 1978): 117–19, a special issue published in conjunction with the society's 1978 World Congress held in Adelaide, Australia.

4. Walter Kaufmann, *The Future of the Humanities* (New York: Thomas Y. Crowell, 1977).

5. R. A. Smith, *The Sense of Art* (New York: Routledge, 1989), 169–83. Cf. Peter Shaw, "Devastating Developments Are Hastening the Demise of Deconstructionism," *Chronicle of Higher Education* 28 November, 1990, B1–2; M. J. Wilsmore, "Against Deconstructing Rationality in Education," *Journal of Aesthetic Education* 25 (Winter 1991): 99–113; and Martin Schralli, "Reconstructing Literary Value," *Journal of Aesthetic Education* 25 (Winter 1991): 115–19.

6. Kaufmann, *The Future of the Humanities*, 70.

7. Kaufmann, "The Art of Reading," in *The Future of the Humanities*, 47–83.

8. Francis Haskell, "Museums and Their Enemies," *Journal of Aesthetic Education* 19 (Summer 1985): 21.

9. Kaufmann, "The Art of Reading," 64.

10. Lionel Trilling, "Mind in the Modern World," in *The Last Decade: Essays and Reviews, 1965–1975*, ed. Diana Trilling (New York: Harcourt Brace Jovanovich, 1977), 122–23. Delivered as the first Thomas Jefferson Lecture in the Humanities of the National Endowment of the Humanities, 1973.

11. Irving Howe, "On Lionel Trilling: 'Continuous Magical Confrontation,'" *The New Republic*, 13 March 1976, 30.

12. Lionel Trilling, "Why We Read Jane Austen," in *The Last Decade*, 204–25.

13. Clifford Geertz, "'From the Native's Point of View': On the Nature of Anthropological Understanding," *Bulletin of the American Academy of the Arts and Sciences* 28 (October 1974): 30, quoted by Trilling in "Why We Read Jane Austen," 216.

14. Clifford Geertz, "Person, Time, and Conduct in Bali," in *The Interpretation of Cultures* (New York: Basic Books, 1973), 403.

15. Geertz, "From the Native's Point of View," 35.

16. Trilling, "Why We Read Jane Austen," 225.

17. Mary Ann Raywid, "Pluralism as a Basis for Educational Policy: Some Second Thoughts," in *Educational Policy*, ed. Janice F. Weaver (Danville, Ill.: Interstate, 1975), 81–99; Diane Ravitch, "Multiculturalism: E Pluribus Plures," *The American Scholar* 59 (Summer 1990): 337–54; Edward Rothstein, "The New Musical Correctness and Its Mistakes," *The New Republic*, 4 February 1991, 29–34; John Wilson, "Art, Culture, and Identity," *Journal of Aesthetic Education* 18 (Summer 1984): 89–97.

18. Raywid, "Pluralism as a Basis for Educational Policy," 92; subsequent references to specific pages will be given in the text.

19. Ravitch, "Multiculturalism: E Pluribus Plures," 338; subsequent references to specific pages will be given in the text.

20. Diane Ravitch, "Multiculturalism: An Exchange," *The American Scholar* 60 (Spring 1991): 272–76.

21. Diane Ravitch, "Multiculturalism in the Curriculum," *Network News and Views* 9 (March 1990): 9 (from a presentation made before the Manhatten Institute, 29 November 1989).

22. Rothstein, "The New Musical Correctness and Its Mistakes," 33–34; subsequent references to specific pages will be given in the text.

23. Bruno Nettl, *The Study of Ethnomusicology* (Urbana: University of Illinois Press, 1983), 305, quoted by Rothstein, 31.

24. John Wilson, "Art, Culture, and Identity," 90; subsequent references to specific pages will be given in the text.

25. A good introduction to this literature for educators is Donald Crawford, "The Questions of Aesthetics," in *Aesthetics and Arts Education*, ed. Ralph A. Smith and Alan Simpson (Urbana: University of Illinois Press, 1991), 18–31.

26. Arthur Schlesinger, Jr., *The Disuniting of America* (New York: Norton, 1992); Midge Decter, "E Pluribus Nihil: Multiculturalism and Black Children," *Commentary* 92 (September 1991): 25–29. In warning that it is a mistake to make a virtue out of alienation, Decter writes that "whatever was the case with their ancestors, they [black children] are the legitimate heirs of a common culture in which the disparate racial and ethnic groups living here come together as Americans, sharing the same national traditions and speaking the same language, and that this common culture must be the name of their desire" (29).

Chapter 6: The Arts, General Knowledge, and Curriculum

1. For Harry S. Broudy's discussions of general education, the arts and the humanities, and the uses of schooling, see *Democracy and Excellence in American Secondary Education*, with B. Othanel Smith and Joe R. Burnett (1964; repr. with new preface, Melbourne, Fla.: R. E. Krieger Publishing Co., 1978); *Enlightened Cherishing: An Essay on Aesthetic Education* (Urbana: University of Illinois Press, 1972); *Truth and Credibility: The Citizen's Dilemma* (New York: Longman, 1981); *The Role of Imagery in Learning* (Los Angeles: Getty Center for Education in the Arts, 1987); *The Uses of Schooling* (New York: Routledge, 1988); and two essays: "A Common Curriculum in Aesthetics and Fine Arts," in *Individual Differences and the Common Curriculum*, ed. Gary D. Fenstermacher and John I. Goodlad, eighty-second yearbook of the National Society for the Study of Education,

part 1 (Chicago: University of Chicago Press, 1983), 219–47, and "Cultural Literacy and General Education," in *Cultural Literacy and Arts Education*, ed. Ralph A. Smith (Urbana: University of Illinois Press, 1991), 7–16.

2. Broudy, "Cultural Literacy and General Education," 11; subsequent references to specific pages will be given in the text.

3. Broudy, *Truth and Credibility*, 137.

4. The antecedents and disciplines of discipline-based art education are discussed in a number of essays in Ralph A. Smith, ed., *Discipline-Based Art Education: Origins, Meaning, and Development* (Urbana: University of Illinois Press, 1989).

5. Albert William Levi, *The Humanities Today* (Bloomington: Indiana University Press, 1970).

6. Albert William Levi and Ralph A. Smith, *Art Education: A Critical Necessity* (Urbana: University of Illinois Press, 1991).

7. R. A. Smith, "Aesthetic Education: A Role for the Humanities Program," *Teachers College Record* 69 (January 1968): 343–54.

8. See R. A. Smith: *Excellence in Art Education: Ideas and Initiatives*, rev. ed. (Reston: National Art Education Association, 1987), *The Sense of Art: A Study in Aesthetic Education* (New York: Routledge, 1989), (with Levi) *Art Education: A Critical Necessity*, and (with coeditor Bennett Reimer) *The Arts, Education, and Aesthetic Knowing*, ninety-first yearbook of the National Society for the Study of Education, part 2 (Chicago: University of Chicago Press, 1992).

9. Levi, *The Humanities Today*, 14–15.

10. Levi, "The Humanities through the Arts," unpublished material, available through R. A. Smith.

11. Levi, *The Humanities Today*, 59–63; subsequent references to specific pages will be given in the text.

12. Jacques Barzun, "Art and Educational Inflation," *Journal of Aesthetic Education* 12 (October 1978): 200. Cf. Monroe C. Beardsley, "Putting Down Words: Some Vicissitudes of Language," *College English* 35 (1974): 740–49.

13. The following discussion of phases of aesthetic learning is drawn, with editing and additions, from Levi and Smith, *Art Education: A Critical Necessity*, 190–207.

14. Kenneth Clark, *Looking at Pictures* (New York: Holt, Rinehart and Winston, 1960), 15–18. Cf. Marcia M. Eaton, *Aesthetics and the Good Life* (Rutherford, N.J.: Farleigh Dickinson University Press, 1989), 110.

15. See Broudy, *The Role of Imagery in Learning*, 49–53.

16. *Toward Civilization: A Report on Arts Education* (Washington: National Endowment for the Arts, 1988).

17. Some standard histories of art are: H. W. Janson, *History of Art*, 3d ed., revised and expanded by Anthony F. Janson (Englewood Cliffs: Prentice-Hall,

1986); Helen Gardner, *Art Through the Ages*, 9th ed., revised by H. de la Croix, Richard G. Tausey, and Diane Kirkpatrick (Chicago: Harcourt Brace Jovanovich, 1987); E. H. Gombrich, *The Story of Art*, 13th ed. (New York: E. P. Dutton, 1978); Hugh Honour and John Fleming, *The Visual Arts: A History*, 2d ed. (Englewood Cliffs: Prentice-Hall, 1986); Frederick Hartt, *Art: A History of Painting, Sculpture, and Architecture*, 3d ed. (New York: H. N. Abrams, 1989). Cf. "The Tradition of Art: Art History," in Levi and Smith, *Art Education: A Critical Necessity*.

18. I have in mind the attention given by arts educators to Howard Gardner's *Frames of Mind* (New York: Basic Books, 1983). I do not assume that Gardner subscribes to all the extrapolations others have made from his theory of multiple intelligences. He does, however, believe that creative activities should be the cornerstone of arts education, which is what I question. See his "Toward More Effective Arts Education," in *Aesthetics and Arts Education*, ed. Ralph A. Smith and Alan Simpson (Urbana: University of Illinois Press, 1991), 274–85.

19. Max Lerner, *America as a Civilization*, 2d ed. (New York: Henry Holt, 1987), 1008. Cf. Lerner, "Myth American," *The New Republic*, 7 September 1987, 11–13.

20. F. David Martin and Lee Jacobus, *The Humanities through the Arts*, 3d ed. (New York: McGraw-Hill, 1983).

21. See Smith, *Excellence in Art Education*, chap. 2.

22. See note 17.

23. Jakob Rosenberg, *On Quality in Art: Criteria of Excellence, Past and Present* (Princeton: Princeton University Press, 1967).

24. Sherman E. Lee, *Past, Present, East and West* (New York: George Braziller, 1983).

25. Kenneth Clark, *What Is a Masterpiece?* (New York: Thames and Hudson, 1979).

26. Martin S. Dworkin, "Seeing for Ourselves: Notes on the Movie Art and Industry, Critics, and Audiences," *Journal of Aesthetic Education* 3 (July 1969): 45–46; Stanley Kauffmann, "Film," in *Quality: Its Image in the Arts*, ed. Louis Kronenberger (New York: Atheneum, 1969), 374–78.

27. Harold Osborne, "Assessment and Stature," and Nelson Goodman, "When Is Art?" both in *Aesthetics and Arts Education*, ed. Ralph A. Smith and Alan Simpson (Urbana: University of Illinois Press, 1991).

28. H. Gene Blocker, *The Aesthetics of Primitive Art* (New York: University Press of America, 1994), chap. 5.

29. Benjamin Rowland, Jr., *Art in East and West: An Introduction through Comparisons* (Cambridge: Harvard University Press, 1954); subsequent references to specific pages will be given in the text.

30. Jacques Maquet, *The Aesthetic Experience: An Anthropologist Looks at the Arts* (New Haven: Yale University Press, 1986).

31. Thomas Munro, *Oriental Aesthetics* (Cleveland: Press of Western Reserve University, 1965).

32. The reference is given by Monroe C. Beardsley in his "Aesthetic Experience Regained," in *The Aesthetic Point of View: Selected Essays*, ed. Michael J. Wreen and Donald M. Callen (Ithaca: Cornell University Press, 1982), 89. For two perceptive analyses of some recent controversies referred to, see Hilton Kramer, "Is Art Above the Laws of Decency?" and Louis E. Lankford "Artistic Freedom: An Artworld Paradox," both in *Public Policy and the Aesthetic Interest*, ed. Ralph A. Smith and Ronald Berman (Urbana: University of Illinois Press, 1992). My example of the duelers in cow manure is taken from Jack Burnham, *Great Western Salt Works: Essays on the Meaning of Post-Formalist Art* (New York: George Braziller, 1974), 159–61.

33. Margaret P. Battin, John Fisher, Ronald Moore, and Anita Silvers, *Puzzles about Art: An Aesthetics Casebook* (New York: St. Martin's Press, 1989).

34. Eaton, *Aesthetics and the Good Life*, 9.

Index

Abstract expressionism, 134
Acculturation, 12, 14, 31, 35
Adler, Mortimer, 10
Aesthetic experiences, 62–63, 65
Aesthetic feature, 62
Aesthetic growth, stages of, 75
Aesthetic learning
    critical analysis in, 139–42
    developing historical awareness in,
        128–31
    exemplar appreciation in, 131–39
    perceiving qualitative immediacy in,
        124–26
    perceptual acumen in, 126–28
    phases of, 110
Aesthetic literacy, 69–70
    and cultural literacy, 74–75
Aesthetics, 64
Aesthetic scanning, 127–28
Aesthetic skills, teaching of, 75
Aesthetic understanding, four cs of, 119
Afrocentrism, 98
Agnostic reading, 82, 84–86
Aiken, Henry, 54
Allusionary base of the mind, 111, 112
Alternatives, study of, 77
Amazonian Suya Indians, chants of, 101–2
American Creed, 113

American educational system, unstated
    policy of, in planned amnesia, 37
American Gothic (Wood), 46
American public culture, segments
    of, 24
Anaesthetics, 64
Anderson, Richard, 21, 36
Anthropological point of view of cul-
    ture, 76
Anthropology, elementary insight of, 16
Antihumanitarism as consequences of new
    ethnicity, 94
Anti-individualism as consequences of
    new ethnicity, 94
Applicative uses of learning, 111
Arnheim, Rudolf, 122
Arnold, Matthew, 10
Aronowitz, Stanley, 29–34, 37, 70
Art
    definition of, 105
    distinguishing between traditional and
        nontraditional, 136–37
    need for background knowledge
        about, 45
Art dances, 48, 49–50, 53
Art education
    contributions to quality of life, 65–66
    as instrumental, 65

Art history. *See also* Arts of continuity
    justification for studying, 128–31
    as source of general knowledge, 2
    Western stress of, 130
Artistic statements, 118
Artistic utterances, 118
    history of, 128–29
Art music, 103
Arts
    aesthetic experiences of, 65
    and contextual knowledge, 45–78
    cultural literacy and the teaching of,
        45–46
Arts education
    content-neutral teaching of skills and
        abilities, 7
    creative activities as cornerstones of, 132
    excellence in, 9
    fragmentation of, 9
    Hirsch's ideas for, 45
    humanities-based curriculum for, 14,
        109, 116, 118, 120, 141
    instrumental value of, 119–20
    multicultural dimension for, 75–78, 138
    new cognitivists in, 13
    obligations of, 47
    perception of, 46
    percipience as goal of, 109–10
    process-centered theories of arts
        education, 13, 116
Arts of continuity, 120, 129. *See also* Art
    history
Art world curriculum, 109
Ascriptive rights, 100–101
Assimilation, melting pot theory of, 64
Associative learning, 111, 112–13
Austen, Jane, 88

Background knowledge, 21
    cultural literacy in, 35–36
    need for, in reading, 45
    psychological structure of, 21
Balinese art, 89–90
Ballet, 51, 53
Baryshnikov, Mikhail, 97
Barzun, Jacques, 37, 123–24

Battin, Margaret P., 140
Bennett, William, 34–35
Berenson, Bernard, 124
Berman, Ronald, 66–68
Birth of Venus (Botticelli), 46
Blake, William, 88
Blocker, H. Gene, 135–36
Bloom, Allan, 10, 11, 29, 32, 35
Botticelli, Sandro, 46
Boyer, Ernest, 10
Braque, Georges, 134
Broudy, Harry S., 8, 110–14, 127–28
Bruner, Jerome S., 9

Cain, William E., 33
Canonical knowledge, 11, 15
Cervantes, Miquel de, 2
Cézanne, Paul, 3
    conception of space, 64
Chicago Art Institute, 140
Chunking information, 20
Ciceronian ideal of universal public
        discourse, 25, 28, 31
Civil religion, 23–24
    in national culture, 24
Clark, Kenneth, 124, 127, 134
Clark, Walter, Jr., 71–74, 114
Clausen, Christopher, 39
Cognitive skills, 21
Comprehending listening, 59
Concrete knowledge, decline in, 37
Conservative restoration, 39
Constable, John, 46, 69, 123
Contemporary dance, 51
Content-neutral skills approach
    to arts education, 7
    to music literacy, 59
    to teaching, 27
Content-specific methods of teaching,
        importance of, 8–9
Contextualism, 60–61, 62, 66
Contextual knowledge, 35, 66
    and the arts, 45–78
    and dance as art, 47–54
    and music literacy, 59
    and theater education, 60–61

Core knowledge, 16–17, 42
  teaching of, 15
Council of Nicaea, 5
Courbet, Gustave, 134
Creativeness, 43
Critical thinking, 43
Cubism, 134
Cultural amnesia
  in contemporary education, 130–31
  problems of, 119
Cultural fundamentalism, 98–99
Cultural heritage, great works of, as
    wellspring of general knowledge, 112
Cultural hierarchy of music, 102–3
Cultural literacy
  acquisition of, 36–37
  and aesthetic literacy, 74–75
  aim of, 38
  association with linguistic literacy, 123
  background knowledge in, 35–36
  basic concerns in, 14
  causes of, 15
  contents of, 22–23
  as excessively Eurocentric, 18
  in context of teacher education, 71–74
  core of, 17
  curriculum for, 109, 114
  decline of, 19, 41, 94–95
  definition of, 12, 16, 46
  democracy in, 17
  and feminism, 18–19
  forging national consensus about
    contents of, 12–13
  Hirsch on, 7–28
  integration of contents in lesson
    plans, 27
  levels of knowledge in, 17
  lexicon of, 25
  periphery of, 17
  reception of, 29–44
  redefining and extending, 13
  responsibility for development of,
    72–73
  slippage in minimal, 10
  spheres in, 40
  surface sense of, 52

and the teaching of arts, 45–46
technical research supporting, 19–22
test for, 8
thin sense, 47
Culturally literate citizenry, intellectual
    capacity of, 30–31
Cultural materialism, credibility of, 67
Cultural metaphor, 3
Cultural particularism, 104–5
  as dysfunctional, 97–98
  flaws in arguments for, 96–97
  promotion of, 80
Cultural percipience, 110
  contributions of study of arts and
    humanities to, 113
  development of, 118–19, 120, 122
Cultural percipience curriculum, 109–10,
    119, 124
  cultivating, 122
  general education in, 110
Cultural pluralism, 14
  contributions of, to American civiliza-
    tion, 93–94
  efficacy of, 94
Cultural uniformity, and pluralism, 31
Culture
  anthropological point of view of, 76
  definition of, 105
Culture-free education, 107–8
Curricular specificity, demand for, 133–34
Curriculum
  cultural percipience, 109–10, 119, 122,
    124
  emphasis on mathematics and sciences
    in, 10
  ethnocentric, 95
  experimental, 69
  extensive, 14, 15, 26, 43, 59, 109, 112, 120,
    123, 129
  humanities-based, 14, 109, 116, 118, 120,
    141
  intensive, 15, 26–27, 39–40, 43, 47, 52,
    59, 60, 109, 112, 120, 129
  reforms in, 10
Currier and Ives, 46

Dance
  art, 48, 49–50, 53
  ballet, 51, 53
  contemporary, 51
  disco, 48–49
  ethnic, 48–49, 53
  experimental, 53
  minimal contextual knowledge needed
    for understanding as art, 47
  modern, 51, 53
  schemata about types of, 54
  social, 48, 53
Dante Alighieri, 2
Darwin, Charles, 41
Deconstruction, 81–82, 112
Decter, Midge, 108
de Jouvenal, Bertrand, 40–41
de Kooning, Willem, 134
Design education, experimental curricu-
  lum in, 69
Developmental psychology, 74–75
Dewey, John, 15, 25, 37, 41, 74, 91
Dialectical reading, 82, 86–92
Dialogical aspect of dialectical reading, 86
Dictionary of Cultural Literacy, 45, 111, 126
Discipline-based art education (DBAE),
  115
Disco dancing, 48–49
Divine Comedy, 2
Dogmatic reading, 82, 84
Du Bois, W. E. B., 18
Dworkin, Martin S., 135

Eaton, Marcia Muelder, 61, 66, 77, 80,
  141–42
Ecology of ideas, 40
Education
  academic intellectuals on, 25
  analysis of uses of, 110–11
  culture-free, 107–8
  design, 69
  discipline-based art, 115
Educational conservatism, 15
Educational formalism, 24–25
Educational reform, urgency of practical,
  46–47

Eliot, T. S., 69
Elliott, David, 75–78
Enclavism, rise of in society, 52
Ethnic dance, 48–49, 53
Ethnic enclavism, 101, 104
Ethnic groups, cultural literacy in, 15
Ethnicity
  and multiculturalism, 92–95
  new, 104–5
Ethnocentric curriculum, 95
Eurocentrism in music, 101
Excellence-in-education movement, 9
Exegetical multiculturalism, 82–84
Exegetical reading, 82
Exemplar appreciation, aesthetic learning
  in, 131–39
Experimental curriculum in design
  education, 69
Experimental dance, 51, 53
Explicit knowledge, 73
Extensive curriculum, 14, 15, 26, 43, 59,
  109, 112, 120, 123, 129

Factual knowledge, 57
Feminism, cultural literacy and, 18–19
Fleming, John, 130
Folk art, 102
Folk music, 101, 102, 103
Formalism, romantic educational, 11
Foundation for Cultural Literacy, 42
Fouquet, Jean, 138
Fox-Genovese, Elizabeth, 18–19
Freire, Paulo, 33
Fry, Roger, 124
Fujiwara no Takanobu, 138

Gardner, Helen, 130
Geertz, Clifford, 88–90
General knowledge
  art history as source of, 2
  components of, 3
  in cultural percipience curriculum, 110
  definition of, 2
  shrinkage in the amount of, 7–8
  tradition of, 1–6

Getty Center for Education in the Arts, 115
Ghandi, 18
Gilbert and Sullivan, 47
Gillespie, Patti P., 60–61, 66
Giotto, 134
Giroux, Henry A., 29–34, 37, 70
Gombrich, E. H., 1–6, 7, 111, 112, 122, 129, 130, 131
Goodlad, John, 10
Goodman, Nelson, 135
Gossaert, Jan, 70–71
Graff, Gerald, 33
Guided listening, 123

Haskell, Francis, 83
Herodotus, 18
High culture, 35
Higher education, crisis of humanities in, 81–82
Higher-level thought processes, 43
Hirsch, E. D., 66, 94, 104
    Aronowitz and Giroux's criticisms of, 29–34
    quality of rhetoric, 38
    Scholes's criticism of, 35–37
    theory of education, 39–40
Historical awareness, developing aesthetic learning in, 128–31
Historical knowledge of tradition, need for, in understanding art, 63–64
Historical-philosophical aspect of dialectical reading, 86–87
Hofstadter, Richard, 34
Honour, Hugh, 130
Howe, Irving, 87
Humanities
    crisis of, in higher education, 81–82
    definition of, 117
    distinction between sciences and, 118
    identification of, with liberal arts, 117–18
    purposes of teaching, 81
Humanities-based curriculum, art education in, 14, 109, 116, 120, 141

Iceberg analogy, 73
Iconoclastic controversy, 70–71
Ideas, reception of different types of, 40–41
Identity
    definition of, 105
    and multiculturalism, 105–7
Ideological thinking, abstractions and distortions of, 34, 67–68
Impressionist style, 75
Insular pluralism, 104
Intensive curriculum, 15, 26–27, 39–40, 43, 47, 52, 59, 60, 109, 112, 120, 129
International Society for Education through Art (INSEA), 80
Interpretive uses of learning, 112, 113
Intrinsic value, ambiguity in, 46
Isidore of Seville, 5

Jacobus, Lee, 133
Janson, H. W., 130
Jeffersonian ideal, 37, 42
Jeffersonian pluralism, distinguishing between linguistic pluralism and, 23
Journal of Aesthetic Education, 13, 45
    general mission of, 114
Judgment of Paris, 1, 2

Kauffmann, Stanley, 135
Kaufmann, Walter, 81–82, 86, 104
Kimball, Roger, 79–80
King, Martin Luther, and "I Have a Dream" speech, 24, 37
Kline, Franz, 134
Knowledge. *See also* Learning
    background, 21, 35–36, 45
    canonical, 11, 15
    contextual, 35, 45–78
    core, 15, 16–17, 42
    explicit, 73
    factual, 57
    general, 1–6, 7–8, 110
    tacit, 73, 111, 113
    translinguistic, 11
    world, 16

Language
  and memory, 20–21
  national, 22–23
Learning. *See also* Knowledge
  aesthetic, 110, 124–42
  applicative, 111
  associative, 111, 112–13
  interpretive, 112–13
  psychological assumptions pertaining
    to, 122
  replication of, 110–11
Leavis, F. R., 34, 41–42
Lee, Sherman E., 134–35
Lerner, Max, 133
Levi, Albert William, 115, 117–19, 124, 141
Levinson, Jerrold, 54–59, 60, 66, 77, 123
Liberal arts, identification of humanities
    with, 117–18
Linguistic literacy, association of cultural
    literacy with, 123
Linguistic pluralism, distinguishing
    between Jeffersonian pluralism
    and, 23
Listening
  comprehending, 59
  guided, 123
Literacy skills, content-indifferent,
    how-to-approach to, 11
Long-term memory, 20, 53–54

Macroculture, 63
  distinctions between microculture
    and, 76
Malcolm X, 18
Maquet, Jacques, 138
Marin, John, 138
Martin, F. David, 133
Mathematics, educational emphasis on, 10
Melting pot model
  of assimilation, 64
  of social integration, 65
Memory, 20
  long-term, 20, 53–54
  short-term, 20–21, 53–54

Metaphors
  religious, 2–3
  sources of, 2–3
Michelangelo Buonarroti, 3
Microculture, 63
  distinctions between macroculture
    and, 76
Minimal comprehending listening, and
    musical literacy, 54–55
Minority groups, cultural literacy in, 15
Modern dance, 51, 53
Mona Lisa (da Vinci), 18
Monoliteracy, 23
Multicultural education, six approaches
    to, 77–78
Multiculturalism, 79–108
  agnostic, 84–86
  and arts education, 75–78, 138
  cultural particularism in, 95–99
  dialectical, 86–92
  as educational goal, 18
  exegetical, 82–84
  extremist thinking on, 79–80
  global context of, 79
  identity in, 105–7
  individual, social, and political dimen-
    sions of, 107–8
  music education in, 75–78
  national context of, 79
  and need for scholarly knowledge,
    99–105
  new ethnicity in, 92–95
  normative force of, 76
  as primary educational priority, 23
Munro, Thomas, 138
Music
  art, 103
  character of non-Western, 102
  cultural hierarchy of, 102–3
  Eurocentrism in, 101
  folk, 103
  multicultural view of, 99–105
  politicization of, 101
  variable functions of, 101–2
Musical correctness, 100

Musical literacy
  development of, within traditions,
    61–66
  relevance of schema theory to, 54–59
  role of propositional knowledge in
    developing, 57
Musical understanding, definition of,
  57–58
Musical utterances
  differences between verbal utterances
    and, 57
  understanding, 54
Music education, multicultural concept of,
  75–78
Myrdal, Gunnar, 14, 113

National culture
  connections between development of
    national language and, 22–23
  role of civil religion in, 24
National Endowment for the Arts, 100,
  114
National language
  connections between development of
    national culture and, 22–23
  domains of, 22–23
National literate culture, 31
Nettl, Bruno, 101, 102–3
Nontraditional art, 137

Olds, Clifton, 70–71, 113, 123
Olmstead, Frederick, 18
Osborne, Harold, 135, 138
Owens, Major, 17

Pakistani Sufi music, 102
Panofsky, Erwin, 4
Parsons, Michael, 74–75, 77
Pedagogical value, 77
Peirce, Charles Sanders, 124–25
Perceptual acumen, aesthetic learning in,
  126–28
Percipience as goal of arts education,
  109–10
Percipience curriculum, 109

Pétain, Marshall, 17
Pew Charitable Trusts, 100
Picasso, Pablo, 134
Piranesi, Giovanni Battista, 69
Pluralism, and cultural uniformity, 31
Polanyi, Michael, 111
  theory of, 113
Political liberalism, goals of, 15
Politicization, of music, 101
Postmodern dance, 51
Problem solving, 43
Process-centered theories of arts educa-
  tion, 13, 116
Propositional knowledge, role of, in
  developing musical literacy, 57
Prototype, 21
Puccini, Giacomo, 47

Qualitative immediacy, 124–26
  aesthetic learning perceiving in, 124–26
Quality of life, contributions of art
  education to, 65–66

Raphael Santi, 3, 134
Ravitch, Diane, 92, 94, 95–99, 104–5
Raywid, Mary Ann, 92–95, 104–5, 107
Read, Herbert, 80
Reading, 19, 82
  agnostic, 82, 84–86
  dialectical, 82, 86–92
  dogmatic, 82, 84
  effective, 20
  exegetical, 82
  need for background knowledge in, 45
  skill in, 21–22
Reading comprehension
  levels of, 19–20
  primary associations in, 21
  teaching, 11
Religion, civil, 23–24
Religious metaphors, 2–3
Rembrandt van Rijn, 3
Renaissance art, 114
Renoir, Pierre-Auguste, 75
Replication of learning, 110–11

Revisionists, 39
Richardson, John, 68–71, 123
Rockefeller Foundation, 100
Rockwell, Norman, 65
Romantic educational formalism, 11
Rosenberg, Jakob, 134–35
Rothstein, Edward, 92, 95, 99–105
Rousseau, Jean Jacques, 15, 25, 37, 41
Rowland, Benjamin, 136–37, 138
Rubens, Peter Paul, 2, 3

St. Luke Painting the Virgin (Gossaert),
     70–71, 113, 123
Scheffler, Israel, 77
Schema research, 10, 11, 19
Schemata, 21–22
  about types of dance, 54
Schema theory, 21, 113
  relevance of to musical literacy, 54–59
Schlesinger, Arthur, Jr., 108
Scholes, Robert, 34–37
Sciences, 10
  distinction between humanities and, 118
Scruton, Roger, 41
Sense-making, as function of formal and
     informal learning, 111
Shakespeare, William, 27
Shared knowledge, 11
  link between shared values and, 1
Shared values, link between shared
     knowledge and, 1
Shattuck, Roger, 39
Short-term memory, 20–21, 53–54
Silverman, Ronald, 127–28
Sizer, Theodore, 10
Snow, C. P., 8, 11, 34, 40, 41–44
Social dance, 48, 53
Social integration, melting pot model
     of, 65
Social unity, effect of decline of cultural
     literacy on, 94–95

Socratic aspect of dialectical reading, 86
Sonata form, learning to perceive, 58
Sparshott, Francis, 47–54, 57, 60, 66, 123
Steiner, George, 37–38

Tacit knowing, 73
  theory of, 111, 113
Teacher education, cultural literacy in
     context of, 71–74
Teaching
  content-neutral skills approach to, 27
  content-specific methods of, 8–9
Theater education, 60–61
Tirthankara, Jain, 138
Toynbee, Arnold, 18
Traditional art, 137
Translinguistic knowledge, 11
Trefil, James, 8
Trilling, Lionel, 34, 88, 90–91

Universalism, 95, 99–100

Value differentiations, 102–3
Van Gogh, Vincent, 3
Verbal utterances, differences between
     musical utterances and, 57
Vermeer, Jan, 65
Visual literacy, 68–71

Wells, H. G., 18
Western civilization, suggested creed for,
     5–6
Western tradition of composition,
     criticisms of, 100–101
Wilson, John, 92, 105–7
Winch, Peter, 47
Wittgenstein, Ludwig, 63
Wood, Grant, 46
World knowledge, 16

Ziegfeld, Edwin, 80

RALPH A. SMITH is a professor of cultural and educational policy in the Department of Educational Policy Studies at the University of Illinois at Urbana-Champaign. He is a distinguished fellow of the National Art Education Association and recipient of two of its awards. Among his publications are *The Sense of Art: A Study of Aesthetic Education; Excellence in Art Education;* and *Art Education: A Critical Necessity* (with Albert William Levi). He has also edited *Discipline-based Art Education: Origins, Meaning, and Development; Cultural Literary and Arts Education; Aesthetics and Arts Education* (with Alan Simpson); and *Public Policy and the Aesthetic Interest* (with Ronald Berman). He is the founding editor of the *Journal of Aesthetic Education* and served for seven years as the executive secretary of the Council for Policy Studies in Art Education.